Basics of
RESEARCH METHODOLOGY

NIPA® GENX ELECTRONIC RESOURCES & SOLUTIONS P. LTD.
New Delhi-110 034

www.nipaers.com

Browse, Search, Read & Buy...

Print Books eChapters
eBooks **Publishers**
Forthcoming Subject Catalogues
New Titles

Online Resources on:

- ✓ Current Affairs
- ✓ Reasoning, Logic & Aptitude
- ✓ Competitive Examinations
- ✓ English Language Lab
- ✓ Writing & Pronunciation Tools
- ✓ Personality Development
- ✓ Online Programmes for Professionals
- ✓ Interview Preparation

Pay Using

   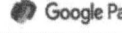   Paytm   CC-Avenue

Basics of
RESEARCH METHODOLOGY

Dr. Ekwal Imam
M. Phil., Ph.D.
P.G.D. Remote Sensing & GIS
Assistant Professor
Department of Biology, Mekelle University
Mekelle, Ethiopia (Africa)

NIPA® GENX ELECTRONIC RESOURCES & SOLUTIONS P. LTD.
New Delhi-110 034

**NIPA® GENX ELECTRONIC
RESOURCES & SOLUTIONS P. LTD.**

101,103, Vikas Surya Plaza, CU Block
L.S.C. Market, Pitam Pura, New Delhi-110 034
Ph : +91 11 27341616, 27341717, 27341718
E-mail: newindiapublishingagency@gmail.com
www: www.nipabooks.com

For customer assistance, please contact
Phone: + 91-11-27 34 17 17
Fax: + 91-11- 27 34 16 16
E-Mail: feedbacks@nipabooks.com

© 2023, Publisher

ISBN: 978-81-19002-82-5

All rights reserved. No part of this publication may be reproduced, stored in a retrieval system or transmitted in any form or by any means, including electronic, mechanical, photocopying recording or otherwise without the prior written permission of the publisher or the copyright holder.

This book contains information obtained from authentic and highly reliable sources. Reasonable efforts have been made to publish reliable data and information, but the author/s, editor/s and publisher cannot assume responsibility for the validity, accuracy or completeness of all materials or information published herein or the consequences of their use. The work is published with the understanding that the publisher and author/s are not attempting to render any professional services. The author/s, editor/s and publisher have attempted to trace and acknowledge the copyright holders of all material reproduced in this publication and apologize to copyright holders if permission and/or acknowledgements to publish in this form have not been taken. If any copyrighted material has not been acknowledged, please write to us and let us know so that we may rectify the error, in subsequent reprints.

Trademark Notice: NIPA®, the NIPA® logos and their presentations (the way they are written/ presented) in this book are the trademarks of the publisher and hence may not be used without written permission, if copied or used without authorization, the infringer will be prosecuted as per law.

NIPA® also publishes books in a variety of electronic formats. Some content that appears in print may not be available in electronic books, and vice versa.

Composed and Designed by NIPA®.

DEDICATED TO

**MY BELOVED
DAUGHTER FATIMA
SON SHARIB
&
WIFE
SHAHINA**

Foreword

It gives me great pleasure to write foreword for the book entitled "Basics of Research Methodology" written by Dr. Ekwal Imam, Assistant Professor of Ecology in the Department of Biology, College of Natural and Computational Science, Mekelle University, Mekelle, Ethiopia.

With the time, Research Methodology has become a very important tool for ecological, natural and medical sciences. Research Methodology has opened up new vistas for biological sciences during twentieth century, however, the subject has not received much attention and there is an extreme paucity of comprehensive and concise text books, which are suitable for students and researchers engaged in ecological and biomedical sciences. Most research outputs fail to gain acceptance at the international level owing to poor research design. Therefore, this book includes some of the widely used procedures and application, which would certainly increase the chances of due recognition of the work.

Many institutions and universities are offering Research Methodology at undergraduate and post-graduate level. But the major challenge is unavailability of basic text books suiting the needs of the countries where English is not their native language. Most of the books on these aspects available in the market are written by authors of western countries and designed to fit into their educational programmes. As a result, there is a need to write a book which should be suitable for students of Asian and African countries, whose mother tongue is not English but their medium of instruction is English.

Dr. Ekwal Imam deserves to be congratulated for his bold effort and devotion for writing this book. Dr. Imam, who was teaching Research Methodology to the Post graduate and Under graduate students in the Department of Biology, Mekelle, University, Ethiopia, has tried to keep the language of this book as simple as possible, so that students from both the continents will have maximum benefit from this book.

I hope this book will surely fill the gap between teachers and taught, on account of its indigenous approach of presentation of the subject matter and immense worth for the biological, biomedical undergraduate, post graduate students and Ph.D. scholars as well.

A copy of this book deserves a space on the shelf of libraries.

Dr.Tesfamichael G. Yohannes
(Ph.D.)
Dean, College of Natural and Computational Science
Mekelle University, Mekelle, Ethiopia (Africa)

Preface

The "Basics of Research Methodology" is a reference book; useful for undergraduates, postgraduates and research scholars of biological, ecological and medical sciences. The book has been written keeping in view the requirements of students at different levels.

Many institutions and universities are offering this course at undergraduate, postgraduate and Ph.D. level. But the major challenge is unavailability of basic text books suiting the needs of the countries where English is not their native language. Most of the books on these aspects available in the market are written by authors of western countries and designed to fit into their educational programmes.

This book grew out of my teaching and research experiences. The purpose of writing this book is to provide an accessible reference book on research methodology, which may be helpful for students in developing proper research design and methodology. The methods described in this book are, of course same as those used in different disciplines, but things are made so user's friendly that even general readers will find this book useful.

The chapters of the book have been organised in such a way that suits the course curriculum of various universities. The book begins with chapter- Introduction, which deals with the concept of research methodology. Second chapter includes details on collection of data, followed by sampling techniques. Chapter four enumerates sample size calculation. Basic concept of probability is provided in chapter five, whereas, in chapter six, hypothesis formulation is discussed in detail. Chapter seven will give an insight on how to write a research proposal/project with an example. In chapter eight, writing a scientific research paper, how to write a review paper, methods of presenting research outcome using oral presentation, poster presentation and ethics in research are discussed. At the end of this chapter, some of the words which are commonly misused are pointed out. Chapter nine is all about the methods deal in data presentation using table, graph, figure etc. A chapter is also devoted to selected bibliography, which may be helpful for further reading.

The material for this book has been drawn from different published and unpublished sources. I do not claim any original contribution except in matters of organization and presentation. While writing this book, various people helped me directly or indirectly. I acknowledge all the authors/publishers mentioned in bibliography, particularly Dunbar, Fienberg, Hutt and Hutt, J. Altman, Jim Fowler & Louis Cohen, R. Kumar, NCERT, Philip N. Lehner, R. Das & P. Das, Salim Javed & Rahul Kaul, and anonymous authors as some of the concepts and examples are taken from their books/write-ups and incorporated here.

I am thankful to my mother Husn Ara, wife Shahina, son Sharib and daughter Fatima for their moral support. Thanks are also acknowledged to Dr. Md. Saghiruddin, Prof. H.S.A. Yahya, Prof Jamal A. Khan, Dr. Afifullah Khan, Prof. Naushad Ahmad, Dr. Satish Kumar, Dr. Orus, Dr. Shahid Ben Zeya, Dr. Khalid Saifullah, Dr. Serajuddin, Dr. Tahir Hussain, Dr. Faiza Abbasi, Dr. Alem, Dr. Sethuraman, Dr. Imtiyaz, Dr. Mushir, Dr. Tadese, Dr. Solomon, Dr. Meheretu, Mr. Zewdneh, Mr. Dawit and Mr. Tsegazeb for their encouragement and valuable suggestions while developing this book. Last but not least at the end I thank publisher, New India Publishing Agency, New Delhi, who agreed to make my dream true.

DR. EKWAL IMAM

Symbols

Common Symbols

α	Alpha: Probability of a type I error
β	Beta: Probability of a type II error
β1	Slope of a regression line
a	Intercept of a regression line on the *y* axis
b	Gradient of a regression line (also known as the regression co-efficient)
β0	Intercept of a regression line
=	Equals
δ	delta: Population mean difference between two paired measurements
≠	Does not equal
≤	Less than or equal to
–	epsilon: The residual or error term in ANOVA and regression
≥	More than or equal to
|a|	Absolute or positive value of a
Σ	Sigma: Summation
θ	theta: The population median or the odds ratio
π	Pi = Population proportion
P(A)	Probability of event A
P(A/B)	Probability of event A given that event B has happened null hypothesis
μ	mu: The population mean
S	Estimate of σ from sample data
Mt	The population trimmed mean
T	T test, critical value that follows the t distribution
N	nu: Degree of freedom
N	Sample size

SD	Sample standard deviation
SE	Sample standard error
ρ	rho: The population correlation coefficient
R	sample correlation
r^2	Coefficient of determination
R^2	Squared multiple correlation in multiple regression
Σ	sigma: The population standard deviation
σ^2	Sigma squared: population variance
Cv	Coefficient of variation
Df	Degree of freedom
ϕ	phi: A measure of association
E	Expected frequency
O	Observed frequency
X	chi: X^2 is a type of distribution
H_0	Null hypothesis
H_1	Alternative hypothesis
$\overline{X}$	X bar: sample mean
Y	Dependent variable in regression
Y'	Predicted value of Y regression
Z	Critical ratio that follows the a z of normal distribution
T	tau: Kendall's tau
P	Probability
U	Test statics of the Mann-Whitney U-test
T	Test statics of the Wilcoxon's test for matched pair
F	Test statics of the F –test
Q	Test statics of the tukey test

Contents

Dedicated to .... *v*
Foreword .... *vii*
Preface .... *ix*
Symbols .... *xi*

1. **Research Methodology** 1
   1.1. Introduction 1
   1.2. Methods of Acquiring Knowledge 2
   1.3. Research Processes 8
   1.4. Summary 10

2. **Collection of Data** 11
   2.1. Introduction 11
   2.2. Primary Data collection Methods 12
      2.2.1. Research, Experiment and Observation 12
      2.2.2. Questionnaire Survey 13
      2.2.3. Interview 18
         2.2.3.1. Personal interview 18
         2.2.3.2. Postal/Mail questionnaire survey 20
         2.2.3.3. Telephone interview 24
      2.2.4. Focus group Interviews 27
      2.2.5. Case-Studies 27
      2.2.6. Diaries 28
   2.3. Summary 29

3. **Sampling Techniques** 31
   3.1. Census and sample surveys 31
   3.2. Classification of Sampling Techniques 37

  3.2.1. Random Sampling 37
  3.2.2. Non-Random Sampling 43
 3.3. Sampling Methods in Ecological Science 48
 3.4. Sampling and Non-Sampling Errors 54
 3.5. Summary 56

4. Sample Size Calculation 57
 4.1. Introduction 57
 4.2. Descriptive Studies 58
 4.3. Analytical Studies 60
 4.4. Survey/Sampling in Ecology 62
 4.5. Summary 63

5. Concept of Probability 65
 5.1. Introduction 65
 5.2. For Single Event 66
 5.3. For Independent Event 66
 5.4. Not Independent Event 67
 5.5. Summary 68

6. Hypothesis Formulation 71
 6.1. Introduction 71
 6.2. Definitions of Hypothesis 72
 6.3. Types of Hypothesis 78
 6.4. Normal Distribution Curve 79
 6.5. Decision Criterion for Accepting or Rejecting
   the Hypothesis 80
 6.6. Two Tailed Tests 82
 6.7. Types of Error 83
 6.8. Summary 87

7. How to Write A Research Proposal 89
 7.1. Introduction 89
 7.2. How to write Research Proposal/Project 90
 7.3. A Typical Format for Research Proposal 94
 7.4. Summary 106

8. Scientific Communication 107
- 8.1. Introduction 107
- 8.2. How to Prepare a Thesis 108
- 8.3. How to Write Scientific Research Paper 116
- 8.4. Writing a Review Paper 124
- 8.5. Oral Presentation 134
- 8.6. Poster Presentation 138
- 8.7. Ethics in Research 145
- 8.8. Commonly Misused Words 148
- 8.9. Summary 151

9. Presentation of Data 153
- 9.1. Introduction 153
- 9.2. Textual Presentation of Data 153
- 9.3. Tabular Presentation of Data 154
- 9.4. Diagrammatic Presentation of Data 158
- 9.5. Maps 176
- 9.6. Summary 178

10. Bibliography 179

Chapter – 1

Research Methodology

Studying this chapter will enable us:
- *To know what research is*
- *To know how to acquire knowledge*
- *To know different types of Research*

1.1. INTRODUCTION

The word *research* derives from the French **"recherche"**, which means to search closely. Research is a process of investigation. It is an examination of a subject from different points of view. It's not just a trip to the library to pick up a stack of materials, or picking the first five hits from a computer search. Research is a hunt for the truth. It is getting to know a subject by reading up on it, playing with the ideas, choosing the areas that interest you and following up on them. Research is the way you educate yourself.

Research can be defined as the search for knowledge or any systematic investigation to establish facts. The primary purpose for research is discovering, interpreting, and the development of methods and systems for the advancement of human knowledge on a wide variety of scientific matters of our world and the universe. Research can use the scientific method, but always not necessary.

Scientific research relies on the application of the scientific method, a harnessing of curiosity. This research provides scientific information and theories for the explanation of the nature and the properties of the world around us. It makes practical applications possible. Scientific research can be subdivided into different classifications according to their academic and application disciplines.

Some Definitions

Research is an attempt to find out or know about in a systematic and scientific manner.

It is a systematic investigation to establish facts

It inquires into.

In research "Scientists are exploring the nature of consciousness.

It is an inquiry: a search for knowledge.

The term *research* is also used to describe an entire collection of information about a particular subject.

1.2. METHODS OF ACQUIRING KNOWLEDGE

Definition of Knowledge

Knowledge is nothing but acquiring the information or getting the information. Knowledge is the primitive stage of knowing anything. It does not require any analysis or research. However, a scientist attempts to gain knowledge through the scientific method.

How to Acquire Knowledge

People have used many methods to gain knowledge:

i. By reason and logic (perhaps in cooperation with others, using logical argument).

ii. By mathematical proof.

iii. By the scientific method.

iv. By the trial and error method.

v. By applying an algorithm.

vi. By learning from experience.

vii. By an argument from authority, this could be from religious, literary, political, philosophical or scientific authorities.

viii. By listening to the testimony of witnesses.

ix. By observing the world in its "natural state"; seeing how the world operates without performing any experiments.

x. By acquiring knowledge that is embedded in one's language, culture, or traditions.
xi. By dialogical enquiry (conversation).
xii. By some claimed form of enlightenment following a period of meditation. (For example, the Buddhist enlightenment known as bodhi)
xiii. By some claimed form of divine illumination or revelation from a divine agency.

Types of Knowledge

Prior knowledge

Knowledge can be classified into a priori knowledge, which is obtained without observing the world.

Posteriori or empirical knowledge

Posteriori or empirical knowledge can only be obtained after observing the world or interacting with it in some way.

Inferential knowledge

Inferential knowledge is based on reasoning from facts or from other inferential knowledge such as a theory. For example, all knowledge about the atom is inferential knowledge. The distinction between factual knowledge and inferential knowledge has been explored by the discipline of general semantics.

Knowledge in Various Disciplines

There are many different disciplines that generate beliefs that can be regarded as knowledge. They include science (which generates scientific theories), law (which generates verdicts), history (which generates historical narratives), and mathematics (which generates proofs).

Inductive Reasoning

Inductive reasoning, also known as **induction** or **inductive logic,** is a type of reasoning that involves moving from a set of specific facts to a general conclusion. It can also be seen as a form of theory-building, in which specific facts are used to create a theory that explains relationships between the facts and allows prediction of future knowledge. The premises of an inductive logical argument indicate some degree of support (inductive probability) for the conclusion but do not entail it; i.e. they do not ensure its truth. Induction is used to ascribe properties or relations to types based on an observation instance (i.e., on a number of observations or experiences); or to formulate laws based on limited observations of recurring phenomenal patterns. Induction is employed, for example, in using specific propositions such as:

This ice is cold. (Or: All ice I have ever touched has been cold.)

This billiard ball moves when struck with a cue. (Or: Of one hundred billiard balls struck with a cue, all of them moved.)

...to infer general propositions such as:

All ice is cold.

All billiard balls move when struck with a cue.

Another example would be:

3+5=8 and eight is an even number. Therefore, an odd number added to another odd number will result in an even number.

Strong and Weak Induction

Strong Induction

All observed crows are black.

Therefore:

All crows are black.

This exemplifies the nature of induction: inducing the universal from the particular.

A strong induction is thus an argument in which the truth of the premises would make the conclusion probable, but not necessitates it as being factual.

Weak Induction

I always hang pictures on nails.

Therefore:

All pictures hang from nails.

Assuming the first statement to be true, this example is built on the certainty that "I always hang pictures on nails" leading to the generalization that "All pictures hang from nails". However, the link between the premise and the inductive conclusion is weak.

In both of these examples of weak induction, the logical means of connecting the premise and conclusion (with the word "therefore") are faulty, and do not give us a strong inductively reasoned statement.

Deductive Reasoning

Deductive reasoning is used in research to establish hypotheses. Deductive reasoning arrives at a specific conclusion based on generalizations. Deductive reasoning is reasoning that involves a hierarchy of statements or truths. Starting with a limited number of simple statements or assumptions, more complex statements can be built up from the more basic ones.

Deductive reasoning can be described as reasoning of the form if A then B. Deduction is in some sense the direct application of knowledge in the production of new knowledge.

If-then deductive reasoning is how scientists (and other people) can test alternate hypotheses. Making deductions is important when we cannot directly observe a cause, and can only observe its consequences. This kind of reasoning can be modeled by the following:

If ...

Then...

But...

Therefore...

For example, we might hypothesize that "The color of a mineral is determined by its crystal structure."

And so we could test this hypothesis using deductive reasoning:

If the color of a mineral is determined by its crystal structure; then all purple minerals should have the same crystal structure. But purple amethyst has a hexagonal structure and purple fluorite has an isometric structure (determined by observations). Therefore, the hypothesis is not supported or strengthened.

Inductive reasoning is essentially the opposite of deductive reasoning.

Again the distinction between the two types of reasoning is not always sharp

Many people distinguish between two basic kinds of argument. Induction is usually described as moving from the specific to the general, while deduction begins with the general and ends with the specific; arguments based on experience or observation are best expressed inductively, while arguments based on laws, rules, or other widely accepted principles are best expressed deductively.

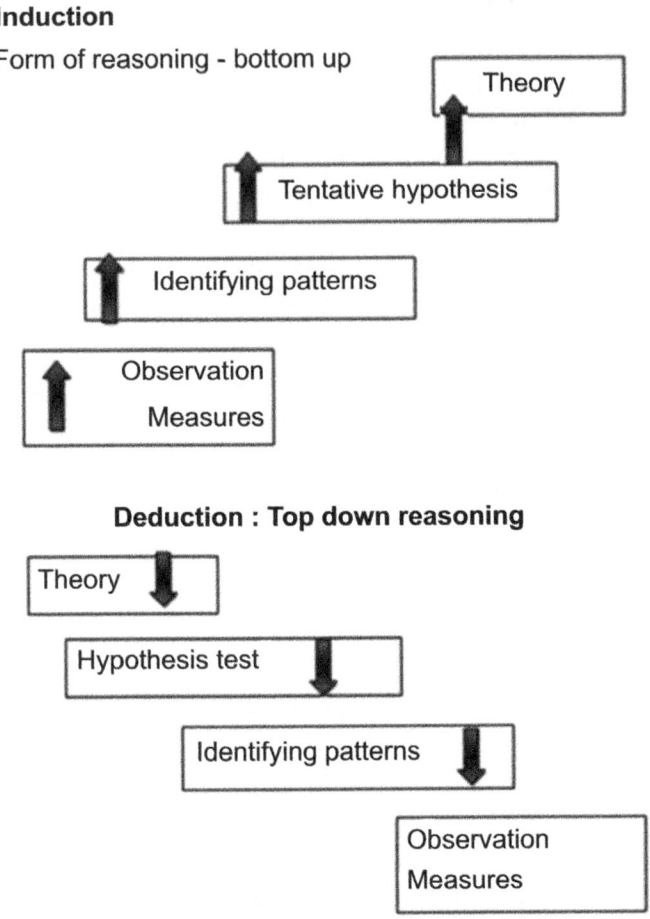

Scientific Methods of Acquiring Knowledge

Scientific methods of acquiring knowledge are very systematic and follow different hierarchical steps. Scientific methods of acquiring knowledge are consists of following major steps:

I. Making Observation
II. Formulating hypothesis
III. Testing
IV. Coming to a conclusion

Research Methodology

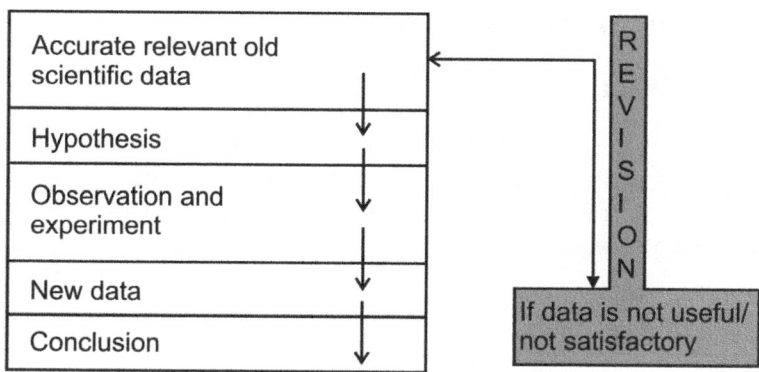

Scientist employs an approach for gathering information using scientific method. On the basis of data (factual information) a scientist formulates a tentative statement (hypothesis). Hypothesis guide further observation. The scientific method involves inductive reasoning. Inductive reasoning is used by scientist to isolate facts to arrive at a general idea. This may explain a phenomenon. For example: Scientist not only observed the prevalence of dark coloured peppered moths on trees in polluted areas, they also observed the prevalence of light coloured peppered moths on trees in non-polluted areas. This caused them to formulate the hypothesis the "predatory birds were responsible for the un-equal distribution of these moths, because birds feed on the moths they can see.

Once a hypothesis has been stated a deductive reasoning comes into play. Deductive reasoning begins with a general statement that infers a specific conclusion. It often takes the form of an: IF, ...THEN........STATEMENT

For example: **IF** predator birds are responsible for unequal distribution of dark and light coloured moths, **THEN**, it will be possible to get evidence of birds feeding primarily on light coloured moth..

Example

Steps	Scientific methods	Applied by a scientist named-Kettlewell
1	observation	Saw more dark moths in polluted area and more light moths in non-polluted area.
2	Hypothesis	Predator birds are responsible for this unequal distribution
3	Experimentation	Released equal number of both types of moths, observe predatory birds, collect and count surviving moth
4	Conclusion	Hypothesis is supported by data

1.3. RESEARCH PROCESSES

Scientific Research

Generally, research is understood to follow a certain structural process. Though step order may vary depending on the subject matter and researcher, the following steps are usually part of most formal research, both basic and applied:

- Formulation of a topic
- Hypothesis
- Conceptual definitions
- Operational definition
- Gathering of data
- Analysis of data
- Test, revising of hypothesis
- Conclusion, iteration if necessary

Different Types of Research

Basic research

Basic research is a type of research that involves investigation of theoretical issues to add to the scientific knowledge base. While this type of research contributes to our understanding of the human mind and behavior, it does not necessarily help solve immediate practical problems.

Basic research is fundamental or *pure* research. Basic research is driven by a scientist's *curiosity* or interest in a scientific question. The main motivation is to *expand man's knowledge,* not to create or invent something. There is no obvious commercial value to the discoveries that result from basic research.

For example, basic science investigations probe for answers to questions such as:

- How did the universe begin?
- What are protons, neutrons, and electrons composed of?
- How do slime molds reproduce?
- What is the specific genetic code of the fruit fly?

Basic research lays down the *foundation* for the applied science. Basic research refers to study and research on pure science that is meant to increase our scientific knowledge base.

The term basic research refers to study and research on pure science that is meant to increase our scientific knowledge base. This type of research is often purely theoretical with the intent of increasing our understanding of certain phenomena or behavior but does not seek to solve or treat these problems.

Examples of basic research

Our understanding of genetics and heredity is largely due to the studies of Gregor Mendel, who studied pea plants in the 1860's, and the experiments with fruit flies by T.H. Morgan in the early 20th century. These organisms were used because it was easier to design experiments using pea plants and fruit flies than using higher forms of life.

Many of today's electrical devices (e.g., **radios**, generators and alternators) can trace their roots to the basic research conducted by Michael Faraday in 1831. He discovered the principle of electromagnetic induction, that is, the relationship between electricity and magnetism.

Applied research

Applied research is a type of research that focuses on solving practical problems. Rather than focusing on developing or investigating theoretical questions, applied research are interested in finding solutions to problems that impact daily life.

Applied research refers to scientific study and research that seeks to solve practical problems. Applied research is used to find solutions to everyday problems, cure illness, and develop innovative technologies. Psychologists working on human factors or industrial/organizational fields often do this type of research.

Applied research is designed to solve *practical problems* of the modern world, rather than to acquire knowledge for knowledge's sake. One might say that the goal of the applied scientist is to *improve the human condition*.

For example, applied researchers may investigate ways to:
- improve agricultural crop production
- treat or cure a specific disease
- improve the energy efficiency of homes, offices, or modes of transportation

Some scientists feel that the time has come to shift from purely basic research to applied science. This trend, they feel, is necessitated by the problems resulting from global overpopulation, pollution, and the overuse of the earth's natural resources.

Applied research is an original or critical investigation undertaken to gain new scientific or technical knowledge with respect to a specific practical objective. For example, any testing in the search for a product alternative would generally be classified as applied research. It is the 'specific practical objective' that distinguishes applied research from pure research.

Example of applied research

Discovery of Vaccinations: Vaccinations against various diseases save countless lives each year. The first use of a vaccine occurred in the late 1790's. Edward Jenner developed a technique for vaccinating people against smallpox, a disease that once killed millions of people. In 1885, Louis Pasteur successfully inoculated a patient with a rabies vaccine, Jonas Salk developed a vaccine for polio in 1953 and; an oral form of the vaccine was produced by Albert Sabin in 1961.

Discovery of Transistor: Prior to the 1950's, vacuum tubes were used as triodes in electrical devices such as radios. In 1948, 3 researchers at AT & T's Bell Laboratories (John Bardeen, Walter Brattain, and William Shockley) invented the transistor, a solid state triode that revolutionized the electronics industry. No doubt, the transistor made possible the invention of the integrated circuit (the key component in microprocessors) by Jack Kilby ten years later.

1.4. SUMMARY

Research can be defined as the search for knowledge or any systematic investigation to establish facts.

Knowledge is nothing but acquiring the information or getting the information.

There are two types of knowledge
- Prior knowledge
- Inferential knowledge

Reasoning is of two types
- Inductive reasoning
- Deductive reasoning

Research may be of following types
- Basic Research
- Applied research

Chapter – 2

Collection of Data

Studying this chapter will enable us:
- To understand the meaning and purpose of data collection
- To distinguish between primary and secondary sources
- To know the mode of data collection

2.1. INTRODUCTION

The purpose of collecting data is to collect evidence for reaching a sound and clear solution to a problem. In this chapter we will study the sources of data, mode of data collection and its techniques.

Sources and Types of Data

Statistical data can be obtained from two sources:

(i) Primary and
(ii) Secondary

The enumerator (person who collects the data) may collect the data by conducting an enquiry or an investigation or experiment. Such data are called Primary Data, as they are based on first hand information. Thus, the data are considered to be primary when it is collected and processed for the first time.

If the data have been collected and processed (scrutinized and tabulated) by some other agency and used by another agency, such type of data are called Secondary Data. Generally, Secondary Data is collected from already published data. Secondary data can be obtained either from published sources or from any other sources like a web site, scientific journals, books, reports, etc.

2.2. PRIMARY DATA COLLECTION METHODS

In primary data collection, we collect the data ourselves using methods such as experiments, observations, interviews and questionnaires. The key point here is that the data we collect is unique to us and our research and, until we publish, no one else has access to it. There are many methods of collecting primary data and the main methods include:

2.2.1. Research, Experiment and Observation

Research is a systematic investigation in order to establish facts and reach new conclusions. It is used to discover or verify information presented. A research may be based on laboratory experiment or observation of nature or natural objects in the field. It may be combination of both; laboratory experiment and field observation.

Experiment is a scientific procedure undertaken to make a discovery, test a hypothesis, or demonstrate a known fact. It is a course of action tentatively adopted without being sure of the outcome. Scientific experiment is done try out new things.

Observation is defined as the action or process of closely observing or monitoring things or animal species or nature. It is the ability to notice significant details of an object or living things. Observation involves recording the behavioural patterns of people, objects and events in a systematic manner. Observational methods may be: structured or unstructured, disguised or undisguised, natural or contrived, Personal, mechanical, non-participant, participant, with the participant taking a number of different roles.

Structured or unstructured observation

In structured observation, the researcher specifies in detail what is to be observed and how the measurements are to be recorded. It is appropriate when the problem is clearly defined and the information needed is specified.

In unstructured observation, the researcher monitors all aspects of the phenomenon that seem relevant. It is appropriate when the problem has yet to be formulated precisely and flexibility is needed in observation to identify key components of the problem and to develop hypotheses.

The potential for bias is high. Observation findings should be treated as hypotheses to be tested rather than as conclusive findings.

Disguised or undisguised: In disguised observation, respondents are unaware that they are being observed and thus behave naturally. Disguise is achieved by hiding, or using hidden equipment.

In undisguised observation, respondents are aware they are being observed. Therefore, it is possible that people / animal behave differently when being observed.

Natural or contrived: Natural observation involves observing behaviour as it takes place in the environment. In contrived observation, the respondents' behaviour is observed in an artificial environment.

Personal: In personal observation, a researcher observes actual behaviour as it occurs. The observer may or may not normally attempt to control or manipulate the phenomenon being observed. The observer merely records what takes place.

Mechanical: Mechanical devices (video, closed circuit television) record what is being observed. These devices may or may not require the respondent's direct participation. They are used for continuously recording on-going behaviour.

Non-participant: The observer does not normally question or communicate with the people being observed. He or she does not participate.

Participant: In participant observation, the researcher becomes, or is, part of the group that is being investigated. Participant observation has its roots in ethnographic studies (study of man and races) where researchers would live in tribal villages, attempting to understand the customs and practices of that culture. It has a very extensive literature, particularly in sociology (development, nature and laws of human society) and anthropology (physiological and psychological study of man). Organisations can be viewed as 'tribes' with their own customs and practices.

The role of the participant observer is not simple. There are different ways of classifying the role: Researcher as employee, Researcher as an explicit role, Interrupted involvement and Observation alone.

2.2.2. Questionnaire Survey

Preparation of questionnaire

The most common type of instrument used in surveys is questionnaire/ interview schedule. The questionnaire is either self administered by the respondent or administered by the researcher (enumerator) or trained investigator. While preparing the questionnaire/interview schedule, we should keep in mind the following points:

- The questionnaire should not be too long. The number of questions should be as minimum as possible. Long questionnaires discourage people from completing them.
- The questionnaire should start from general questions and proceed to more specific ones. This helps the respondents feel comfortable. Write the name of respondent after finishing the questionnaire sheet, so that he may not feel scared.

    Poor Questionnaire
    (i) Is increase in electricity charges justified?
    (ii) Is the electricity supply in your locality regular?

    Good Questionnaire
    (i) Is the electricity supply in your locality regular?
    (ii) Is increase in electricity charges justified?

- The questions should be precise and clear.

    Poor Questionnaire

    What percentage of your income do you spend on clothing in order to look presentable?

    Good Questionnaire

    What percentage of your income do you spend on clothing?

- The questions should not be ambiguous, to enable the respondents to answer quickly, correctly and clearly.

    Poor Questionnaire

    Do you spend a lot of money on books in a month?

    Good Questionnaire

    Q. How much do you spend on books in a month?
    I. Less than Rs 200
    II. Between Rs 200-300
    III. Between Rs 300-400
    IV. More than Rs 400

- The question should not use double negatives. The questions starting with "Wouldn't you" or "Don't you" should be avoided, as they may lead to biased responses. For example:

  Poor Questionnaire

  Don't you think smoking should be prohibited?

  Good Questionnaire

  Do you think smoking should be prohibited?

- The question should not be a leading question, which gives a clue about how the respondent should answer. For example:

  Poor Questionnaire

  How do you like the flavour of this high-quality tea?

  Good Questionnaire

- How do you like the flavour of this tea?

The question should not indicate alternatives to the answer. For example:

Poor Questionnaire

Would you like to do a job after college or be a housewife?

Good Questionnaire

Would you like to do a job, if possible?

Types of questions

Closed ended or structured questionnaire

Questions can either be a two-way question or a multiple choice question. When there are only two possible answers, 'yes' or 'no', it is called a two way question. When there is a possibility of more than two options of answers, multiple choice questions are more appropriate. In this, a question is asked and then a number of possible answers are provided for the respondent. The respondent selects the answer which is appropriate.

Example,

Q. Why did you sell your land?

   (i) To pay off the debts.

   (ii) To finance children's education.

   (iii) To invest in another property.

   (iv) Any other (please specify).

Closed ended questions are easy to use because all the respondents have to respond from the given options. But on the other hand they are difficult to write as the alternatives should be clearly written to represent both sides of the issue. There is also a possibility that the individual's true response is not present among the options given. For this, the choice of 'Any Other' is provided, where the respondent can write a response, which was not anticipated by the researcher. Moreover, another limitation of multiple-choice questions is that they tend to restrict the answers by providing alternatives, without which the respondents may have answered differently. However, closed questions are particularly useful in obtaining factual information. Foe Example:

Sex: Male [ ] Female [ ]

Did you watch television last night?   Yes [ ] No [ ]

Some 'Yes/No' questions have a third category 'Do not know', but experience shows that if this alternative is not mentioned people will make a choice. Apart from this, the phrase 'Do not know' is ambiguous:

Do you agree with the introduction of the EMU?

Yes [ ] No [ ] Do not know [ ]

What was your main way of travelling to the hotel? Tick one box only.

Car   [ ]
Coach   [ ]
Motor bike   [ ]
Train   [ ]
Other means, please specify —

With such lists you should always include an 'other' category, because not all possible responses might have been included in the list of answers.

Sometimes the respondent can select more than one from the list. However, this makes analysis difficult:

Why have you visited the historic house? Tick the relevant answer(s). You may tick as many as you like.

I enjoy visiting historic houses   [ ]

The weather was bad and I could not enjoy outdoor activities [ ]

I have visited the house before and wished to return   [ ]

Other reason, please specify

Collection of Data

Attitude questions

Frequently questions are asked to find out the respondents' opinions or attitudes to a given situation. A Likert scale provides a battery of attitude statements. The respondent then says how much they agree or disagree with each one:

Read the following statements and then indicate by a tick whether you strongly agree, agree, disagree or strongly disagree with the statement.

	Strongly agree	Agree	Disagree	Strongly disagree
There should be an option for Right to Reject in voter machine				

There are many variations on this type of question. One variation is to have a 'middle statement', for example, 'Neither agree nor disagree'. However, many respondents take this as the easy option. Only having four statements, as above, forces the respondent into making a positive or negative choice. Another variation is to rank the various attitude statements; however, this can make analysis more difficult.

Which of these characteristics do you like about your job? Indicate the best three in order, with the best being number 1.

Varied work	[4]
Good salary	[2]
Opportunities for promotion	[1]
Good working conditions	[3]
High amount of responsibility	[6]
Friendly colleagues	[5]

A semantic differential scale attempts to see how strongly an attitude is held by the respondent. With these scales double-ended terms are given to the respondents who are asked to indicate where their attitude lies on the scale between the terms. The response can be indicated by putting a cross in a particular position or circling a number:

Work is: (circle the appropriate number)

Difficult 1 2 3 4 5 6 7 Easy
Useless 1 2 3 4 5 6 7 Useful
Boring 1 2 3 4 5 6 7 Interesting

The semantic differential (difference in words meaning) can provide a useful way of measuring and summarizing subjective opinions.

Other types of questions to determine peoples' opinions or attitudes are:

    Which one/two words best describes...?
    Which of the following statements best describes...?
    How much do you agree with the following statement...?

Open questions/questionnaire

Open-ended questions allow for more individualized responses, but they are difficult to interpret and hard to score, since there are a lot of variations in the responses.

Example,

Q. What is your view about Globalisation?

An open question such as 'What are the essential skills a manager should possess?' should be used as an adjunct to the main theme of the questionnaire and could allow the respondent to elaborate upon an earlier more specific question. Open questions inserted at the end of major sections, or at the end of the questionnaire, can act as safety valves, and possibly offer additional information. However, they should not be used to introduce a section since there is a high risk of influencing later responses. The main problem of open questions is that many different answers have to be summarised and possibly coded.

2.2.3. Interview

There are three basic mode of data collection:

2.2.3.1. Personal interview

This method is used when the researcher has access to all the members. The researcher (or investigator) conducts face to face interviews with the respondents. Personal interviews are preferred due to various reasons. Personal contact is made between the respondent and the interviewer. The interviewer has the opportunity of explaining the study and answering any query of the respondents. The interviewer can request the respondent to expand on answers that are particularly important. Misinterpretation and misunderstanding can be avoided. Watching the reactions of the respondents can provide supplementary information.

Collection of Data

Interviewing is a technique that is primarily used to gain an understanding of the underlying reasons and motivations for people's attitudes, preferences or behaviour. Interviews can be undertaken on a personal one-to-one basis or in a group. They can be conducted at work, at home, in the street or in a shopping centre, or some other agreed location.

Advantages of interviews

Serious approach by respondent resulting in accurate information. Interview provides good response rate, completed and immediate responses and possible in-depth questions. Interviewer can give help if there is a problem and can investigate motives and feelings. Interviewer can use recording equipment. Characteristics of respondent can be assessed - tone of voice, facial expression, hesitation, etc.

Disadvantages of interviews

It is time consuming. It has Geographic limitations. It can be expensive. Normally need a set of questions. Respondent may be bias - tendency to please or impress, create false personal image, or to end interview quickly. Embarrassment possible if personal questions are asked. Transcription and analysis can present problems.. If there are many interviewers, training required, which is a costly affair.

Types of interview

Structured interview

It is based on a carefully worded interview schedule. Frequently require short answers with the answers being ticked off. It is useful when there are a lot of questions which are not particularly contentious or thought provoking. Respondent may become irritated by having to give over-simplified answers.

Semi-structured interview

The interview is focused by asking certain questions but with scope for the respondent to express him or herself at length.

Unstructured

This is also called an in-depth interview. The interviewer begins by asking a general question. The interviewer then encourages the respondent to talk freely. The interviewer uses an unstructured format, the subsequent direction of the interview being determined by the respondent's initial reply. The interviewer then probes for elaboration - 'Why do you say that?' or, 'That's interesting, tell me more' or, 'Would you like to add anything else?' being typical probes.

Following are the step-by-step guide to conducting an interview. We should remember that all situations are different and therefore we need refinements to the approach.

Planning an interview

List the areas in which we require information. Decide on type of interview. Transform areas into actual questions. Try them out on a friend or relative. Make an appointment with respondent(s) - discussing details of why and how long. Try and fix a venue and time when we there will be no disturbances.

Conducting an interview

Personally	-	Arrive on time and be smart. smile, employ good manners, find a balance between friendliness and objectivity.
At the start	-	Introduce yourself, re-confirm the purpose, assure confidentiality - if relevant specify what will happen to the data.
The questions	-	Speak slowly in a soft, yet audible tone of voice, control your body language, know the questions and topic, ask all questions.
Responses	-	Record the responses provided by respondent on written questionnaire. Tape recorder can also be used for the same. Proper equipment in good working order should be carried out by interviewer with sufficient tapes and batteries.
At the end	-	Ask if the respondent would like to give further details about anything or any questions about the research, thank them.

2.2.3.2. Postal/Mail questionnaire survey

When the data is going to be collected by mail, the questionnaire is sent to each individual by mail with a request to complete and return it by a given date. The advantages of this method are that, it is less expensive. It allows the researcher to have access to people in remote

Collection of Data

areas too, who might be difficult to reach in person or by telephone. It does not allow influencing of the respondents by the interviewer. It also permits the respondents to take sufficient time to give thoughtful answers to the questions. These days online surveys or surveys through short messaging service i.e. SMS have become popular.

Limitations of mail survey

The disadvantages of mail survey are that, there is less opportunity to provide assistance in clarifying instructions, so there is a possibility of misinterpretation of questions. Mailing is also likely to produce low response rates due to certain factors such as returning the questionnaire without completing it, not returning the questionnaire at all, loss of questionnaire in the mail itself, etc.

Design of postal questionnaires

Theme and covering letter

The general theme of the questionnaire should be made clear in a covering letter. We should state who we are; why the data is required; give, if necessary, an assurance of confidentiality and/or anonymity; and contact number and address. This ensures that the respondents know what they are committing themselves to, and also that they understand the context of their replies. If possible, we should offer an estimate of the completion time. Instructions for return should be included with the return date made obvious. For example: 'It would be appreciated if you could return the completed questionnaire by…...(mention date).

Instructions for completion

We need to provide clear and unambiguous instructions for completion. Within most questionnaires there are general instructions and specific instructions for particular question. It is usually best to separate these, supplying the general instructions as a preamble to the questionnaire, but leaving the specific instructions until the questions to which they apply. The response method should be indicated (circle, tick, cross, etc.).

Appearance of questionnaire

Appearance is usually the first feature of the questionnaire to which the recipient reacts. A neat and professional look will encourage further consideration of our request, increasing response rate. There are a number of simple rules to help improve questionnaire appearance: Liberal spacing makes the reading easier. Photo-reduction can produce more space without reducing content. Consistent positioning of response boxes, usually to the right, speeds up completion and also avoids inadvertent omission of responses. Choose the font style to maximize legibility. Differentiate between instructions and questions. Either lower case or capitals can be used, or responses can be boxed.

Length

There may be a strong temptation to include any vaguely interesting questions, but we should avoid this at all costs. Excessive size can only reduce response rates.

Order

Probably the most crucial stage in questionnaire response is the beginning. Once the respondents have started to complete the questions they will normally finish the task, unless it is very long or difficult. Consequently, we need to select the opening questions with care. Usually the best approach is to ask for biographical details first, as the respondents should know all the answers without much thought. Another benefit is that an easy start encourage respondent to answer the questions. We should be aware of the varying importance of different questions. Essential information should appear early and relatively unimportant questions can be placed towards the end. If questions are likely to provoke the respondent and remain unanswered, these too are best left until the end, in the hope of obtaining answers to everything else.

Coding

If analysis of the results is to be carried out using a statistical package or spreadsheet, it is advisable to code non-numerical responses when designing the questionnaire, rather than trying to code the responses when they are returned. An example of coding is:

Male [ ]	Female [ ]		
1	2		

OR

Variables	Poor	Good	Very good	Excellent
Code	1	2	3	4

The coded responses (1 or 2) are then used for the analysis.

Collection of Data

Thank you

Respondents to questionnaires rarely benefit personally from their efforts, therefore, the least the researcher can do is to thank them. The covering letter should express appreciation for the help given. It is also nice to finish the questionnaire with a further thank you.

Questions

Keep the questions short, simple and to the point and avoid all unnecessary words. Use words and phrases that are unambiguous and familiar to the respondent. For example, 'dinner' has a number of different interpretations; use an alternative expression such as 'evening meal'. Only ask questions that the respondent can answer. Hypothetical questions should be avoided. Avoid calculations and questions that require a lot of memory work, for example, 'How many people stayed in your hotel last year?' Avoid loaded or leading questions that imply a certain answer. For example, by mentioning one particular item in the question, 'Do you agree that Colgate toothpaste is the best toothpaste?' Vacuous words or phrases should be avoided. 'Generally', 'usually', or 'normally' are imprecise terms with various meanings. They should be replaced with quantitative statements, for example, 'at least once a week'. Questions should only address a single issue. For example, questions like: 'Do you take annual holidays to Spain?' should be broken down into two discreet stages, firstly find out if the respondent takes an annual holiday, and then secondly find out if they go to Spain. Do not ask two questions in one by using 'and'. For example, 'Did you watch television last night and read a newspaper?' Avoid double negatives. For example, 'Is it not true that you did not read a newspaper yesterday?' Respondents may tackle a double negative by switching both negatives and then assuming that the same answer applies. This is not necessarily valid. State units required but do not aim for too high a degree of accuracy. For instance, use an interval rather than an exact figure:

'How much did you earn last year?'
Less than Rs.10,000/   [ ]
Rs.10,000 - Rs.20,000/   [ ]

Avoid emotive or embarrassing words - usually connected with race, religion, politics, sex, money.

Testing of pilot survey

Questionnaire may be full of difficulties and problems. A number of rewrites will be necessary, together with refinement. Do not assume that we will write the questionnaire accurately and perfectly at the first attempt. If poorly designed, we will collect inappropriate or inaccurate data and good analysis cannot then rectify the situation.

To refine the questionnaire, we need to conduct a pilot survey. This is a small-scale trial prior to the main survey that tests all our question planning. Amendments to questions can be made. After making some amendments, the new version would be re-tested. If this re-test produces more changes, another pilot would be undertaken and so on. For example, perhaps responses to open-ended questions become closed; questions which are all answered the same way can be omitted and difficult words replaced, etc. It is usual to pilot the questionnaires personally so that the respondent can be observed and questioned if necessary. By trying each question, we can identify any questions that appear too difficult, and we can also obtain a reliable estimate of the anticipated completion time for inclusion in the covering letter. The result can also be used to test the coding and analytical procedures to be performed later.

Distribution and return

The questionnaire should be checked for completeness to ensure that all pages are present and that none is blank or illegible. It is usual to supply a prepaid addressed envelope for the return of the questionnaire. We need to explain this is the covering letter and reinforce it at the end of the questionnaire, after the 'Thank you'.

2.2.3.3. Telephone interview

This is an alternative form of interview to the personal, face-to-face interview. In a telephone interview, the investigator asks questions over the telephone. They allow the researcher to assist the respondent by clarifying the questions. Telephone interview is better in the cases where the respondents are reluctant to answer certain questions in personal interviews.

Advantages of telephone interview

It is relatively cheap and can be completed quickly. It can cover reasonably large numbers of people or organisations. Its geographic coverage is wide. It has high response rate - keep going till the required number is not met. No need to wait. Through this spontaneous response can be achieved. Respondent can be helped in answering. Answers can also be taped.

Disadvantages of telephone interview

The disadvantage of this method is access to people Always you have to recall or remind the respondent and on average 2.5 calls are needed to get someone. Telephone Interviews also obstruct visual reactions of the respondents. Respondent has little time to think. Good telephone manner is required otherwise respondent may feel irritation.

How to start

First you have to locate the respondent. Repeat calls may be necessary especially if we are trying to contact people in organisations where we may have to go through secretaries. We may not know an individual's name or title - so there is the possibility of interviewing the wrong person. We can send an advance letter informing the respondent that we will be telephoning. This can explain the purpose of the research.

Then you have to make respondent agree to take part in interview. We need to state concisely the purpose of the call. It is similar to the introductory letter of a postal questionnaire. Respondents will normally listen to this introduction before they decide to co-operate or refuse. When contact is made respondents may have questions or raise objections about why they could not participate. We should be prepared for these.

Smooth implementation

Interview schedule: each interview schedule should have a cover page with number, name and address. The cover sheet should make provision to record which call it is, the date and time, the interviewer, the outcome of the call and space to note down specific times at which a call-back has been arranged. Space should be provided to record the final outcome of the call - was an interview refused, contact never made, number disconnected, etc.

Procedure for call-backs: a system for call-backs needs to be implemented. Interview schedules should be sorted according to their status: weekday call-back, evening call-back, weekend call-back or, specific time call-back.

Advantages and Disadvantages of Personal interview, mailing question and telephonic interview

Types of Interview	Advantages	Disadvantages
Personal interview	• Highest Response Rate • Allows use of all types of questions • Better for using open-ended questions • Allows clarification of ambiguous questions.	• Most expensive • Possibility of influencing respondents • More time taking.
Mailing questionnaire	• Least expensive • Only method to reach remote areas • No influence on respondents • Maintains anonymity of respondents • Best for sensitive questions.	• Cannot be used by illiterates • Long response time • Does not allow explanation of • unambiguous questions • Reactions cannot be watched.
Telephonic interview	• Relatively low cost • Relatively less influence on respondents • Relatively high response rate.	• Limited use • Reactions cannot be watched • Possibility of influencing respondents.

Comparison of Postal, Telephone and Personal Interview Surveys

The table below compares the three common methods of postal, telephone and interview surveys - it might help us to decide which one to use.

	Postal survey	Telephone survey	Personal interview
Cost (assuming a good response rate)	Often lowest	Usually in-between	Usually highest
Ability to probe	No personal contact or observation	Some chance for gathering additional data through elaboration on questions, but no personal observation	Greatest opportunity for observation, building rapport, and additional probing

Contd...

Respondent ability to complete at own convenience	Yes	Perhaps, but usually no	Perhaps, if interview time is prearranged with respondent
Interview bias	No chance	Some, perhaps due to voice inflection	Greatest chance
Ability to decide who actually responds to the questions	Least	Some	Greatest
Impersonality	Greatest	Some due to lack of face-to-face contact	Least
Complex questions	Least suitable	Somewhat suitable	More suitable
Visual aids	Little opportunity	No opportunity	Greatest opportunity
Potential negative respondent reaction	'Junk mail'	'Junk calls'	Invasion of privacy
Interviewer control over interview environment	Least	Some in selection of time to call	Greatest
Time lag between soliciting and receiving response	Greatest	Least	May be considerable if a large area involved
Suitable types of questions	Simple, mostly dichotomous (yes/no) and multiple choice	Some opportunity for open-ended questions especially if interview is recorded	Greatest opportunity for open-ended questions
Requirement for technical skills in conducting interview	Least	Medium	Greatest
Response rate	Low	Usually high	High

2.2.4. Focus Group Interviews

A focus group is an interview conducted by a trained moderator in a non-structured and natural manner with a small group of respondents. The moderator leads the discussion. The main purpose of focus groups is to gain insights by listening to a group of people from the appropriate target market talk about specific issues of interest.

2.2.5. Case-Studies

The term case-study usually refers to a fairly intensive examination of a single unit such as an animal species, an area, a person, a small group of people, or a single company. Case-studies involve measuring what is there and how it got there. It can enable the researcher to explore, unravel and understand problems, issues and relationships. The case looked at may be unique and, therefore not representative of other instances. It is, of course, possible to look at several case-studies to represent certain features of management that we are interested in studying. The case-study approach is often done to make practical improvements. Contributions to general knowledge are incidental.

The case-study method has four steps:

1. Determine the present situation.
2. Gather background information about the past and key variables.
3. Test hypotheses: The background information collected should be analysed for possible hypotheses. In this step, specific evidence about each hypothesis can be gathered. This step aims to eliminate possibilities which conflict with the evidence collected and to gain confidence for the important hypotheses. The culmination of this step might be the development of an experimental design to test out more rigorously the hypotheses developed, or it might be to take action to remedy the problem.
4. Take remedial action: The aim is to check that the hypotheses tested actually work out in practice. Some action, correction or improvement is made and a re-check carried out on the situation to see what effect the change has brought about.

The case-study enables rich information to be gathered from which potentially useful hypotheses can be generated. It can be a time-consuming process. It is also inefficient in researching situations which are already well structured and where the important variables have been identified. They lack utility when attempting to reach rigorous conclusions or determining precise relationships between variables.

2.2.6. Diaries

A diary is a way of gathering information about the way individuals spend their time on professional activities. They are not about records of engagements or personal journals of thought. Diaries can record either quantitative or qualitative data.

Advantages of Diaries

- Useful for collecting information from employees.
- Different writers compared and contrasted simultaneously.
- Researcher not personally involved.
- Diaries can be used as a preliminary or basis for intensive interviewing.
- Used as an alternative to direct observation or where resources are limited.

Disadvantages of Diaries

- Subjects need to be clear about what they are being asked to do, why and what?
- Diarists need to be of a certain educational level.
- Some structure is necessary to give the diarist focus, for example, a list of headings.
- Encouragement and reassurance are needed as completing a diary is time-consuming and can be irritating after a while.
- Progress needs checking from time-to-time.
- Confidentiality is required as content may be critical.
- Analyses problems, so we need to consider how responses will be coded before the subjects start filling in diaries.

2.3. SUMMARY

Sources and Types of Data
- Primary and
- Secondary

Data can be collected through
- Research
- Experiment and
- Questionnaire Survey

Chapter – 3

Sampling Techniques

Studying this chapter will enable us:
- *To understand the meaning and purpose of sampling*
- *To distinguish between Census and Sample Surveys*
- *To become familiar with the techniques of sampling*

3.1. CENSUS AND SAMPLE SURVEYS

Census or Complete Enumeration

A survey, which includes every element of the population, is known as Census or the Method of Complete Enumeration. If certain agencies are interested in studying the total population of a country, they have to obtain information from all the households in rural and urban area.

The essential feature of this method is that this covers every individual unit in the entire population. We cannot select some and leave out others. We may be familiar with the Census of a country, which is carried out after a particular period like every ten years. A house-to-house enquiry is carried out, covering all households. Human demographic data on birth and death rates, literacy, workforce, life expectancy, size and composition of population, etc. are collected and published by a government agency.

Sample Survey

Population or the Universe in statistics means totality of the items under study. A population is always all the individuals/items who possess certain characteristics (or a set of characteristics). The first task in selecting a sample is to identify the *population*. Once the population is identified, the researcher selects a *Representative Sample*, as it is difficult to study the entire population. *A sample refers to a group or section of the population from which information is to be obtained. A good sample (representative sample)* is generally smaller than the *population* and is capable of providing reasonably accurate information about the population at a much lower cost and shorter time.

Suppose we want to study the average income of people in a certain region. According to the Census method, it would be required to find out the income of every individual in the region, add them up and divide by number of individuals to get the average income of people in the region.

This method would require huge expenditure, as a large number of enumerators have to be employed.

Alternatively, we select a *representative sample,* of a few individuals, from the region and find out their income. The average income of the selected group of individuals is used as an estimate of average income of the individuals of the entire region.

Example

Research problem 1: To study the economic condition of agricultural labourers in a particular region/district.

- *Population*: All agricultural labourers in a particular area.
- *Sample*: Ten per cent of the agricultural labourers in that area.

Research problem 2: To study the crown density of a state's forest.

- *Population:* Crown density of each tree found in that state.
- *Sample:* Ten percent of the forest patch of that state randomly selected.

Some of the Definition

Population or Universe

- The entire group of people, events, or things of interest that the researcher wishes to investigate.

Sample

- A subset of the population.
- A set of cases that is drawn from a larger pool and used to make generalizations about the population.

Sample frame

- A specific list that closely approximates all elements in the population—from this the researcher selects units to create the study sample.

Sample element

- A case or a single unit that is selected from a population and measured in some way—the basis of analysis (e.g., an person, thing, specific time, etc.).
- A single member of the population.

Subject

- A single member of the sample.

Parameter

- Any characteristic of a population that is true → known on the basis of a census (e.g., % of males or females; % of college students in a population).

Estimate

- Any characteristic of a sample that is estimated → estimated on the basis of samples (e.g., % of males or females; % of college students in a sample).

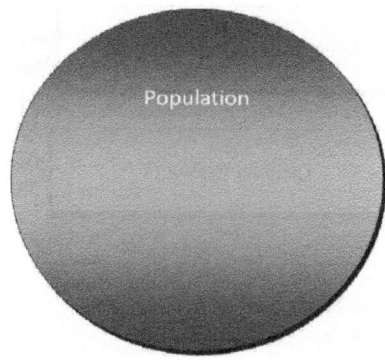

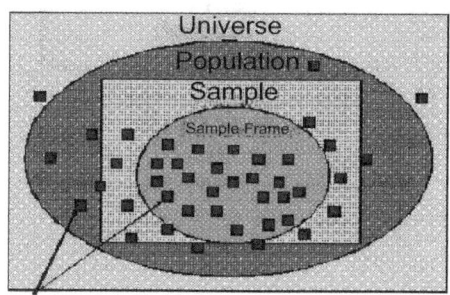

Conceptual Model

Why Sample Survey?

Most of the surveys are sample surveys. These are preferred in statistics because of a number of reasons. A sample can provides reasonably reliable and accurate information at a lower cost and shorter time. As samples are smaller than population, more detailed information can be collected by conducting intensive enquiries. As we need a smaller team of enumerators, it is easier to train them and supervise their work more effectively. Therefore, sampling is suggested for quick results in low budget.

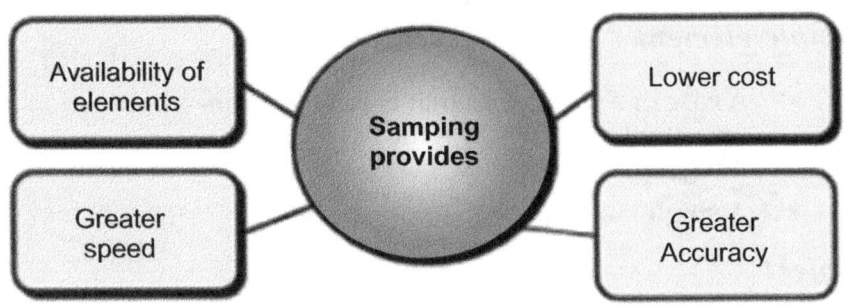

The Sampling Process

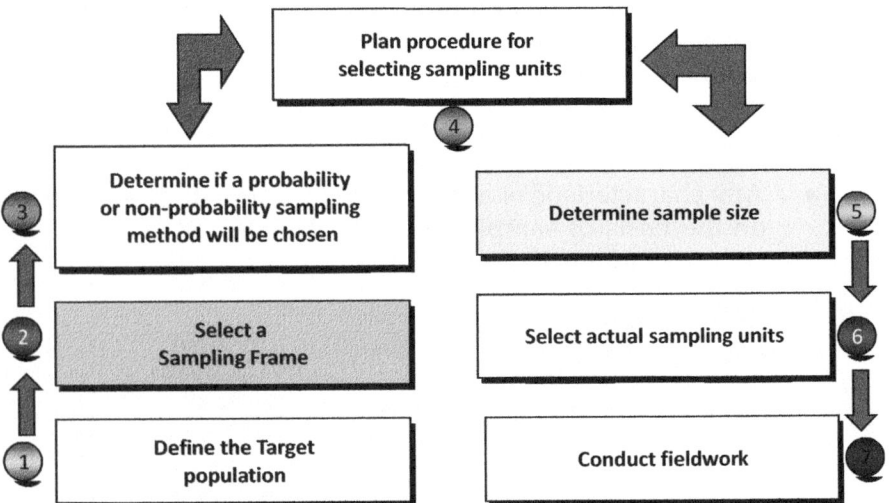

Sample Size

- In general, the larger the sample size (selected with the use of probability techniques) the better is the result. The more heterogeneous a population is on a variety of characteristics (e.g. race, age, sexual orientation, religion) then a larger sample is needed to reflect that diversity.
- Response rates vary on the type of surveys (e.g. mail surveys, telephone surveys). Response rates under 60 or 70 per cent may compromise the integrity of the random sample.

How Good Must the Sample Be ?

- There is no uniform standard of quality that must be reached by every sample.
- The quality of the sample depends entirely on the stage of the research and how the information will be used.

What is the Appropriate Sample Design?

For an appropriate sampling design we have to consider following points:

- Degree of accuracy
- Resources
- Time
- Advanced knowledge of the population
- National versus local issues
- Need for statistical analysis

Representative Sample

A sample should have following characteristics to fulfil its criteria:

- A sample whose characteristics correspond to, or reflect, those of the original population or reference population.
- To ensure representativeness, the sample may be either completely random or stratified depending upon the conceptualized population and the sampling objective (i.e., upon the decision to be made).

Objectives of Sampling

A sampling is done with the following objectives:
To understand:
- Why we use sampling
- Definitions in sampling
- Sampling errors
- Main methods of sampling
- Sample size calculation

To get information from large populations with:
- Reduced costs
- Reduced field time
- Increased accuracy
- Enhanced methods

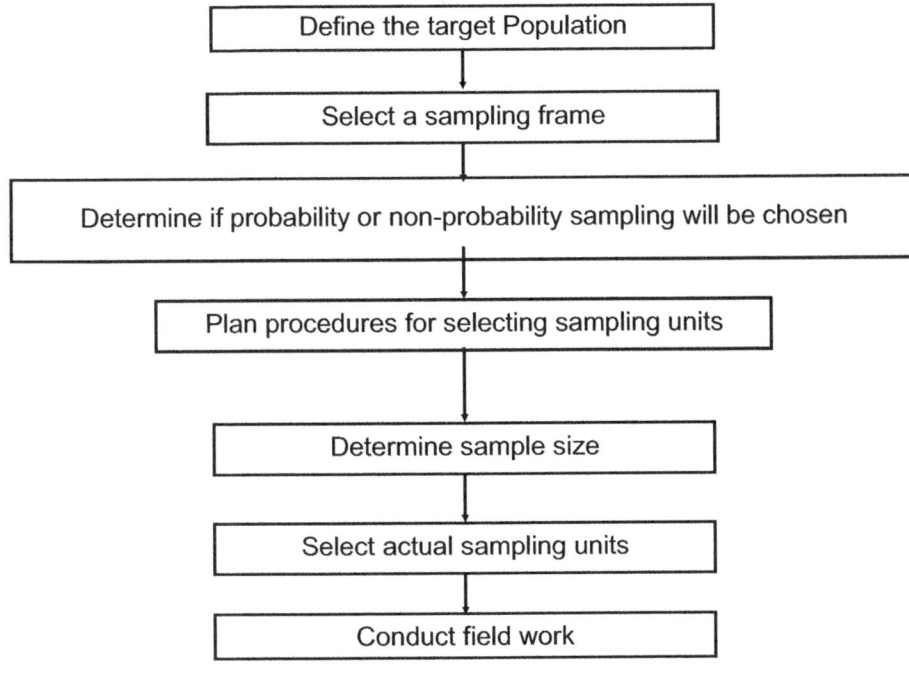

How to design sampling

3.2. CLASSIFICATION OF SAMPLING TECHNIQUES

Sampling techniques are broadly divided into two:
1. Random Sampling
2. Non-random Sampling

3.2.1. Random Sampling

In random sampling an individual unit is selected from the population (samples) randomly. This randomly selected sample unit is representative of population.

Suppose government wants to determine the impact of the rise in petrol price on the household budget of a particular locality. For this, a representative (random) sample (households) has to be taken and studied. For example, consider a village having 300 households.

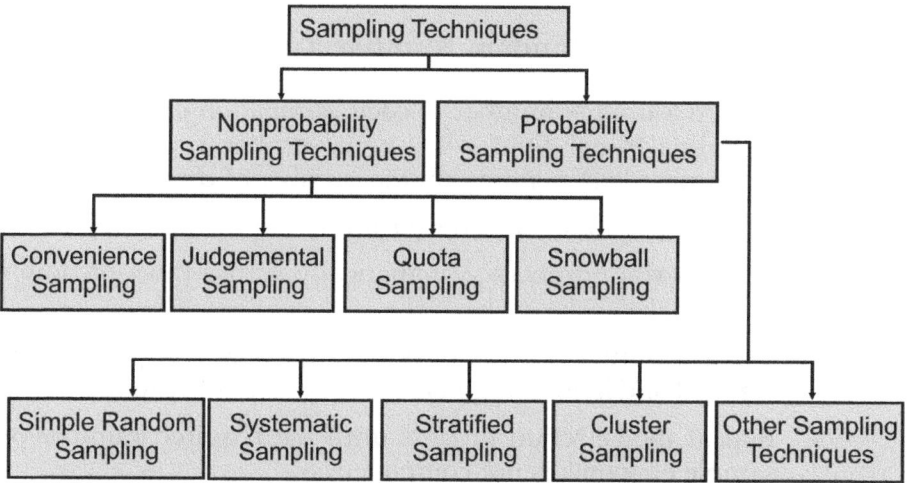

The names of all the 300 households of that area will be written on pieces of paper and mixed well, and then 30 names to be interviewed will be selected one by one.

In the random sampling, every individual has an equal chance of being selected and the individuals who are selected are just like the ones who are not selected. In the above example, all the 300 sampling units (also called sampling frame) of the population got an equal chance of being included in the sample of 30 units and hence the sample, such drawn, is a random sample. This is also called lottery method. The same could be done using a Random Number Table also.

How to use the Random Number Tables?

Random number tables have been generated to guarantee equal probability of selection of every individual unit (by their listed serial number in the sampling frame) in the population.

They are available either in a published form or can be generated by using appropriate software packages. We can start using the table from anywhere, i.e., from any page, column, row or point. In the above example, we need to select a sample of 30 households out of 300 total households. Here, the largest serial number is 300, a three digit number and therefore we consult three digit random numbers in sequence. We will skip the random numbers greater than 300 since there is no household number greater than 300. Thus, the 30 selected households are with serial numbers: 149, 219, 111, 165, 230, 007, 089, 212, 051, 244, 300, 051, 244, 155, 300, 051, 152, 156, 205, 070, 015, 157, 040, 243, 479, 116, 122, 081, 160, and 162.

Steps to be used for Random Number Tables

I. Assign a unique number to each population element in the sampling frame. Start with serial number 1, or 01, or 001, etc. upwards depending on the number of digits required.

II. Choose a random starting position.

III. Select serial numbers systematically across rows or down columns.

IV. Discard numbers that are not assigned to any population element and ignore numbers that have already been selected.

V. Repeat the selection process until the required number of sample elements is not completed.

Types of Random Sampling

1. Simple Random Sampling
2. Stratified Random sampling
3. Multistage Random sampling
4. Multi-phase random sampling

Simple Random Sampling

- Simple random Sampling is one in which sampling units composing the samples are selected by some strictly random process from the whole population without dividing it into homogenous block

- Required sample can be easily drawn with the aid of random number table.
- The tables have been so constructed that every number has an independent and almost equal chance of appearing
- It is best methods of sampling, provided, the population is homogenous
- If population is large it is not likely to be seriously distorted
- If sample size is very small say 30 or less it is likely to be high in error
- In some situation it is not considered good if it is not good representative of various cross section

Simple Random Sampling		
Pupulation	**Sample Method**	**Resulting Sample**
The population identified uniquely by number	Selection by random number	Every member of the population has an equal chance of being selected into the sample

Random Table

	1	2	3	4	5	6	7	8	9	10	11	12	13	14	15	16	17	18	19	20
1	37	75	10	49	98	66	3	86	34	80	98	44	22	22	45	83	53	86	23	51
2	50	91	56	41	52	82	98	11	57	96	27	10	27	16	35	34	47	1	36	8
3	99	14	23	50	21	1	3	25	79	7	80	54	55	41	12	15	15	3	68	56
4	70	72	1	00	33	25	19	16	23	58	3	78	47	43	77	88	15	2	55	67
5	18	46	6	49	47	32	58	8	75	29	63	66	89	9	22	35	97	74	30	80
6	65	76	34	11	33	60	95	3	53	72	6	78	28	14	51	78	76	45	26	45
7	83	76	95	25	70	60	13	32	52	11	87	38	49	1	82	84	99	2	64	00

8	58	90	7	84	20	98	57	93	36	65	10	71	83	93	42	46	34	61	44	1
9	54	74	67	11	15	78	21	96	43	14	11	22	74	17	2	54	51	78	76	76
10	56	81	92	73	40	7	20	5	26	63	57	86	48	51	59	15	46	9	75	64
11	34	99	6	21	22	38	22	32	85	26	37	00	62	27	74	46	2	61	59	81
12	2	26	92	27	95	87	59	38	18	30	95	38	36	78	23	20	19	65	48	50
13	43	4	25	36	00	45	73	80	2	61	31	10	6	72	39	2	00	47	6	98
14	92	56	51	22	11	6	86	88	77	86	59	57	66	13	82	33	97	21	31	61
15	67	42	43	26	20	60	84	18	68	48	85	00	00	48	35	48	57	63	38	84

Advantages of Simple Random Sampling

- Easy to implement
- Sampling error easily measured

Disadvantages of Simple Random Sampling

- Time consuming
- High cost
- Complete accounting of population needed
- Cumbersome to provide unique designations to every population member
- Very inefficient when applied to skewed population distribution (over- and under-sampling problems) – this is not "overcome with the use of an electronic database)

Stratified Random Sampling

- The stratified random sampling is that method of sampling in which the population is first divided into sub-population of different strata
- In stratified random sampling heterogeneous population has to be divided into smaller homogeneous strata
- Then sampling units are selected from each of them in proportion to their size.
- Divide population of units into groups (called **strata**) and take a simple random sample from each of the strata.

Why We Choose

College survey: Two strata = undergraduate and graduate dormitories.

Sampling Techniques

- Take a simple random sample of 15 rooms from each of the strata for a total of 30 rooms

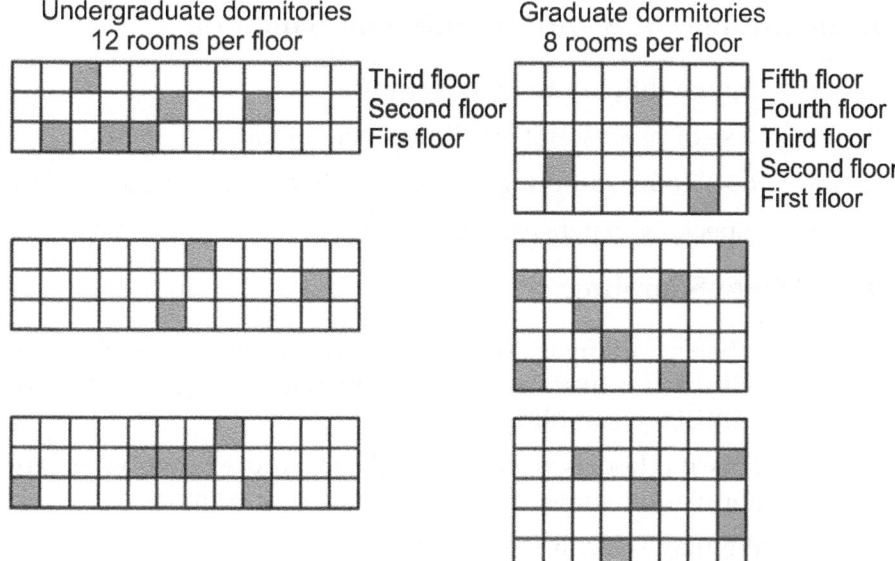

Number of school children in a population

Age in yr	Boys	Girls	Total
5-8	156	148	304
9-12	624	635	1259
13-15	49	52	101
Total	829	835	1664

Stratified sample from population of school children
n=(sample size/total population)* group frequency

Age in yr	Stratified from boys	Stratified from Girls	Total
5-8	(175/1664)*156=16	(175/1664)*148=16	32
9-12	(175/1664)*624=66	(175/1664)*635=67	133
13-15	(175/1664)*49=5	(175/1664)*52= 5	10
Total	87	88	175

Advantages of Stratified Random Sampling

- Can acquire information about the whole population and individual strata
- Precision increased if variability within strata is less (homogenous) than between strata

- Provides data to represent and analyze subgroups
- Enables use of different methods in strata

Disadvantages of Stratified Random Sampling

- Can be difficult to identify strata
- Loss of precision if small numbers in individual strata
- Resolve by sampling proportionate to stratum population
- Especially expensive if strata on population must be created

Multi Stage Sampling

- When sampling is done in stages from bigger to smaller units within the units selected at previous stage, it is called multistage sampling.
- This method is used generally in studies involving large population spread over large state or a country
- We may select a small district in first stage, and then some blocks from the same district, then at 3rd stage select some villages.

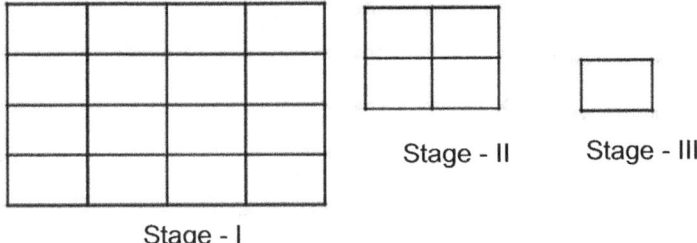

Stage - I   Stage - II   Stage - III

Multi-phase Random Sampling

- In this method some of the same sampling units are used at the different phases (at different time frame) of sampling to collect different information or same information using different method
- Example =for preparing a forest inventory, the volume is estimated on aerial photograph using photo interpretation technique and in the second phase a subset is selected and visited in the field for direct determination of these volumes.

Sampling Techniques

3.2.2. Non-Random Sampling

There may be a situation that we have to select 10 out of 100 households in a locality. We have to decide which household has to be select and which has to be rejected. We may select the households conveniently situated or the households known to us or our friend. In this case, we are using our judgment (bias) in selecting 10 households. The way of selecting 10 out of 100 households is not a random selection. In a non-random sampling method all the units of the population do not have an equal chance of being selected and convenience or judgment of the investigator plays an important role in selection of the sample. They are mainly selected on the basis of judgment, purpose, convenience or quota, so that they are non-random samples.

Types of Non-Random Sampling

1. Selective sampling
2. Systematic sampling
3. Sequential sampling
4. Convenience sampling
5. Purposive sampling
6. Quota Sample

Selective Sampling

- Selective sampling consists of choosing samples according to the subjective judgment of the observer.
- Selective sampling may give good approximations of the population parameter if it is properly used by a person with intensive knowledge of the population.

Systematic Sampling

- Systematic sampling is that method of non-random sampling in which sampling units are selected according to a predetermined pattern.
- Most commonly the pattern envisages regular spacing of units
- For example sampling unit may be located 80 meters apart in rows which may be 200 meters apart in column.
- The selection of the first unit may be random or according to a fixed arbitrary (logical) rule.

- When the first unit is selected at random and others according to a fixed pattern the sampling is referred as systematic sampling with a random start.

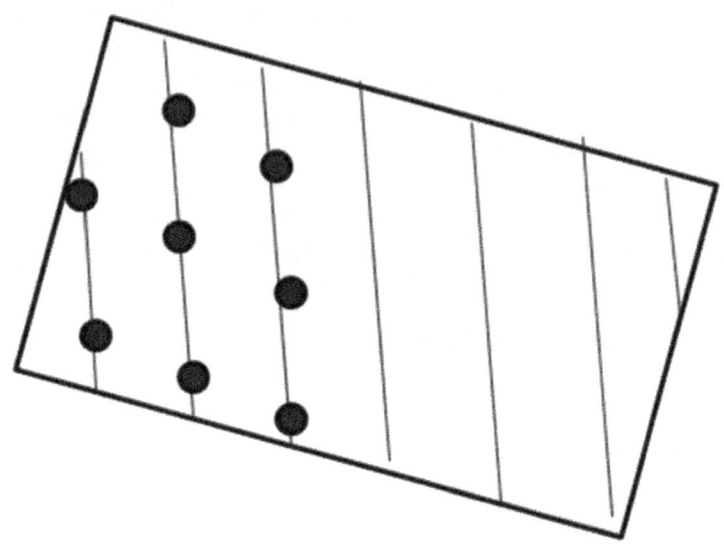

In above figure, distance in row is 80 mts and distance in column is 100mts.

Sequential Sampling

- In this type of sampling the number of observations in the sample is not determined in advance, sampling units are taken successively from a population.
- Sampling is stopped when desired precision is reached.
- Hypothesis is tested each time and a new observation is made to determine whether the hypothesis should be accepted or rejected.
- When hypothesis is tested and accepted or rejected no further sampling is required.

Convenience Sampling

- This is a sampling technique which selects those sampling units most conveniently available at a certain point in, or over a period, of time.

Sampling Techniques

- Major advantages of convenience sampling is that it is quick, convenient and economical; a major disadvantage is that the sample may not be representative.
- Convenience sampling is best used for the purpose of exploratory research and supplemented subsequently with probability sampling
- Very low cost
- Extensively used/understood
- No need for list of population elements
- Disadvantages of this sampling is that the variability and biasness can not be measured or controlled, and projecting data beyond sample not justified.

Purposive / Judgemental Sampling

- In this type of sampling, we select those samples which are having similar specific characteristics
- *Example 1* : The Consumer Price Index (CPI) is based on a judgment sample of market-based items, housing costs, and other selected goods and services which are representative for most of the overall population in terms of their consumption
- *Example 2* : Selection of certain voting districts which serve as indicators for the national voting trend
- Judgment samples require a judgment or an "educated guess" on the part of the interviewer as to who should represent the population. Also, "judges" (informed individuals) may be asked to suggest who should be in the sample.
- In this type of sampling, certain members of the population will have a smaller or no chance of selection compared to others
- It involves selecting a group of people because they have particular traits that the researcher wants to study, e.g. consumers of a particular product or service in some types of market research
- Sample will meet a specific objectives ant cost involved in this type of technique is moderate
- The results may be biased

Quota Sample

- The sampling procedure that ensure that a certain characteristic of a population sample will be represented to the exact extent that the investigator desires
- This is a sampling technique in which the business researcher ensures that certain characteristics of a population are represented in the sample to an extent which is he or she desires
- Example: A business researcher wants to determine through interview, the demand for Product X in a district which is very diverse in terms of its ethnic composition. If the sample size is to consist of 100 units, the number of individuals from each ethnic group interviewed should correspond to the group's percentage composition of the total population of that district
- Quota sampling is two-stage restricted judgmental sampling. The first stage consists of developing control categories, or quotas, of population elements. In the second stage, sample elements are selected based on convenience or judgment.

Characteristic Sex	Population	Quota Percentage	Sample Percentage
Male	480	10	48
Female	520	10	52
	1000	10	100

- It is widely used in opinion polls and market research.
- Interviewers given a quota of subjects of specified type to attempt to recruit.

  eg. an interviewer might be told to go out and select 20 male smokers and 20 female smokers so that they could interview them about their health and smoking behaviours .
- Advantages of Quota sampling include the speed of data collection, less cost, the element of convenience, and representativeness (if the subgroups in the sample are selected properly)
- It is very extensively used and understood

Sampling Techniques

Snowball Sampling

- It is a sampling technique in which individuals or organizations are selected first by probability methods, and then additional respondents are identified based on information provided by the first group of respondents
- Example: Through a sample of 500 individuals, 20 diving enthusiasts are identified which, in turn, identify a number of other divers

In snowball sampling, an initial group of respondents is selected, usually at random.

After being interviewed, these respondents are asked to identify others who belong to the target population of interest.

Subsequent respondents are selected based on the referrals.

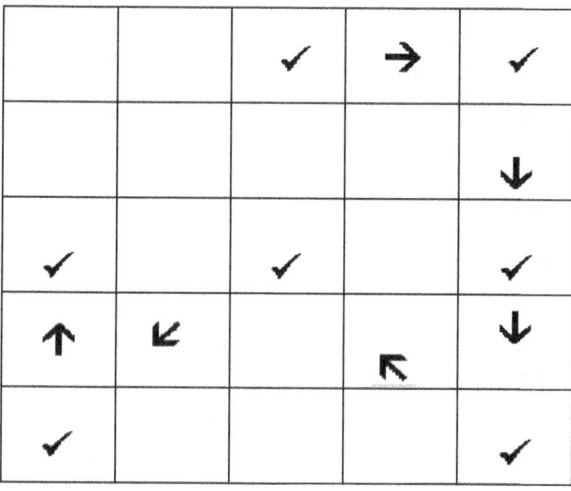

- Snowball sampling is often used for populations that are not easily identified or accessed; and involves building a sample through referrals, i.e.) you identify someone from your population willing to be in your study. You then ask them to identify others who meet the study criteria. Each of those individuals is then asked for further recommendations
- It is Low cost
- Useful in specific circumstances
- Useful for locating rare populations

3.3. SAMPLING METHODS IN ECOLOGICAL SCIENCE

The sampling methods discussed over here are based al-most entirely on Altmann (1974) review. The sampling method we select for our research should be based on

i. Our research question and research objectives,

ii. The behavioral units we have selected to measure,

iii. Our experimental design, and

iv. A multitude of practical considerations, such as availability of equipment, animals, visibility, etc.

Following are some of the methods used for ecological samplings:

Random vs. Haphazard Samples

Random sample

It is a sample drawn from a population in such a way that all possible samples have the same probability of being selected.

(e.g., prescribed sample, assigned numbers and then drawn from a hat).

Haphazard samples

In this sampling, samples are taken on some arbitrary basis, generally convenience.

(e.g. sample, taken before lunch and after lunch) or when the animals are thought to be most active.

True random sampling is often difficult in the field situation; but the researcher must consciously attempt to attain randomization through unbiased sampling efforts.

Ad *Libitum* Sampling

In *ad libitum* method, no restraints are employed in sampling behavior. What is recorded are generally the behaviors of those individuals (or groups) that are most easily observed. It is like "typical field notes." Altmann (1974) states that "In field studies of behavior *ad libitum* sampling is perhaps the most common form of behavior record".

Ad libitum sampling is most often used when an ethologist merely recording as much as he can, during i) an unplanned encounter with a species or ii) during reconnaissance observations for a later study.

Since it is rare that all individuals are equally visible, some researchers have attempted to measure individual. At some regularly scheduled time period (*e.g.,* half hour intervals) censuses were taken of the individuals which were visible.

Sociometric Matrix

A *sociometric matrix* is really an experimental design or a way of tabulating data. Collection of data for a sociometric matrix can be considered as special type of all occurrence sampling in which the observer searches for interactions between pairs of individuals (*e.g.,* transmitter-receiver, Groomer-groomee) or records interactions by an individual (focal animal) during a specified sampling period.

Suppose we want to study the relationship among seven male individuals of the same group to establish dominance hierarchism among them. For this we have to record dyadic interaction of competitive feeding, grooming, approach, withdrawal, threats and submissions and all these events will be classified into two categories i.e. win or lose. An individual was considered to win if he was able to fetch food from other, groomed by other, approached by other, withdrawal of other on his arrival and showing threats to other (by chasing, biting, showing bare teeth). If the responses were recorded opposite, it was considered that individual had lost the competition. All these can be done by using socio-metric.

Matrix showing dominance order of adult males in Achaltal monkey Group (during 1993)

Individuals	UP	FH	RE	WL	HF	WF	CN
UP		1	1	1	1	1	1
FH	0		1	0	1	1	1
RE	0	0		0	1	1	1
WL	0	0	1		1	0	1
HF	0	0	0	0		1	1
WF	0	0	0	1	0		1
CN	0	0	0	0	0	0	

Male in the vertical row on the left was dominant to the male in the horizontal top row,

Most dominant animal on top left.

1= Win, 0 =loose

The above matrix reflects the following result:

Male dominancy in Achaltal monkey group (during 1993)

Individual	Dominates on
UP	FH, WL, HF, WF, RE, CN
WL	HF, RE, CN
FH	HF, WF, RE, CN
HF	WF, CN
WF	WL, CN
RE	HF, WF, CN
CN	00

Above Tables show the status of win/lose of different adult males. It was found that "UP" male was most dominant and defeated all other males present in the group. On the second position "FH" was present which always won from other four individuals (HF, WF, RE, and CN). On the third ranking position "RE" as well as "WL" were present, as both used to defeat three members of the group. "RE" defeated HF, WF and CN, while WL male was victorious compared to HF, WF and CN. The dominance rank of HF and WF was same (third) as they used to defeat WF, CN, WL and CN respectively. CN acquired last ranking position as all other group members defeated this monkey.

Focal-Animal Sampling

In this method, one individual is the focus of observations during a particular sample period. A particular individual receives highest priority for recording its behavior, but it does not necessarily restrict us to only that individual. Where social behavior is recorded, a focal-animal sample on an individual provides a record of all acts in which that animal is either the actor or receiver (Altmann 1974). It is necessary to record the length of each sample period and the amount of time that the focal animal is in view during that period. The problem of all animal under observation temporarily disappearing from view has not been successfully resolved. There is no valid procedure for determining (predicting) what behavior(s) occurred while that animal was out of sight. Four methods for dealing with this problem are discussed below relative to the duration of behaviors and time out of sight. Although none of these methods is valid, the hazards in using them can be reduced by following the guidelines:

Sampling Techniques

For out-of-sight periods of long duration and when the durations of common behaviors are short (relative to the out-of-sight periods) do the following:
  i. Delete the time out of sight from the sample; duration of the sample period is reduced accordingly.
  ii. Delete the time out of sight from the sample, but increase observation time until the time the animal was actually observed equals the time required for the predetermined sample period.

For out-of-sight periods of short duration and when the duration of common behaviors are long (relative to the out-of-sight periods) do this:
  i. Assign the behavior seen when the animal goes out of sight to the out-of sight period.
  ii. Assign the behavior seen when the animal comes back into view to the out-of-sight period.

Behaviors occupying the largest percentage of the animal's time budget are those that are most likely to be interrupted. Two factors which should, perhaps, override or dictate use of the above methods are experience and common sense. Probably no one knows the animal better than you do; therefore follow the course of action which you consider to be the most appropriate. Also, it is often wise to deal with data using two or more methods for comparison.

All Occurrences

It may be desirable to focus on one or a limited number of behaviors and record all occurrences [called "event-sampling" by Hutt and Hutt (1974) and "complete record" by Slater (1978)]. This contrasts with focal-animal sampling where the focus is on the individual. All occurrences of selected behavior is possible if the following factors exist:
  i. Observational conditions are adequate.
  ii. The behaviors have been carefully defined so that they are easily recognized.
  iii. The behaviors do not occur more often (or more rapidly) than the observer can record them.

This method of sampling can provide the following types of information:

i. Rate of occurrence (and temporal changes in rate) of the selected behavior(s);

ii. Restricted sequencing.

iii. Behavioral synchrony.

Sequence Sampling

In sequence sampling the focus is on a chain of behaviors. These may be performed by a single individual (e.g. courtship displays in male ducks, or they may be behaviors alternating between two (or more) individuals (e.g., courtship in the queen butterfly).

The initiation of a sample period is usually determined by the beginning of a sequence. An experience observer can often anticipate the initiation of a sequence in an individual and an impending interaction between two or more individuals. The sample period terminates when the observed sequence terminate.

There may be difficulty in specifying the beginning and end of a sequence, as well as choosing individual sequences or social interactions at random.

One-Zero Sampling

One-zero sampling is a method in which the observer scores whether a behavior occurs (one) or not (zero) during a short interval of time (sample period). It is suitable for recording states and/or events. This method is often referred to in the literature as "time-sampling" (Hutt and Hutt 1974) or *the* "Hansen system" (Fienberg 1972).

This method has the following features:

i. In each sample period the occurrence or nonoccurrence (not frequency of occurrence) is scored.

ii. Behaviors of one or more individuals are recorded in each sample period.

iii. Occurrence refers to either an event or a state (ongoing at some point during the sample period).

iv. Sample periods are generally short *(e.g.,* 15 seconds), and several *(e.g.,* 20) are used in succession.

Caution should be used when converting one-zero Scores to percent of time spent in a behavior (Simpson and Simpson 1977). This would be correct only if the behavior lasted for the complete sample periods in which it was scored. Slater (1978) suggests that one -zero data may be used as a first-approximation look at associations between behaviors, by determining how frequently they occur in the same time unit as each other.

The major disadvantage of this sampling method is that a large amount of information about frequency and duration is lost. The researcher has to weigh this disadvantage against the case of scoring and high inter observer reliability which this method provides.

Instantaneous and Scan Sampling

Instantaneous sampling is a special type of one-zero sampling in which the observer scores an animal's behavior at predetermined "points" in time (called "time-sampling" by Hutt and Hutt 1974). This method has also been termed "point" sampling by Dunbar (1976) and "on -the-dot" sampling by Slater (1978). This method can be used to obtain data on the time distribution on behavioral states in an individual.

Scan sampling is simply a form of instantaneous sampling in which several individuals are "scanned" at predetermined points and their behavioral states are scored. The same sample point can be used as in instantaneous sampling. Behavior categories chosen for study should be clearly delineated to assist in quick scoring. Estimates of time spent scanning individuals, as well as -groups, should be made. One important use of instantaneous and scan sampling is to estimate the percentage of time that individuals spend in various activities (e.g., time budgets).

Sampling methods and recommended uses (Altmann1974).

Sampling methods	State or event sampling	Recommended uses
Ad libitum	Either	Primarily of heuristic value; suggestive records of rare but significant events.
Sociometric matrix competition	Event	Asymmetry within dyads.
Focal -animal	Either	Sequential constraints percentage of time; rates; durations; nearest neighbor relationships.
All occurrences of selected behaviors	Usually event	Synchrony rates
Sequences	Either	Sequential constraints
One -zero	Usually state	None
Instantaneous and scan	State	Percentage of time synchrony sub groups.

3.4. SAMPLING AND NON-SAMPLING ERRORS

Sampling Errors

The purpose of the sample is to take an estimate of the population. Sampling error refers to the differences between the sample estimate and the actual value of a characteristic of the population (that may be the average income, etc.). It is the error that occurs when we make an observation from the sample taken from the population. Thus, the difference between the actual value of a parameter of the population (which is not known) and its estimate (from the sample) is the sampling error. It is possible to reduce the magnitude of sampling error by taking a larger sample.

Example

Consider a case of incomes of 5 farmers of an area. The variable x (income of farmers) has measurements 500, 550, 600, 650, 700. We note that the population average of (500+550+600+650+700) ÷ 5 = 3000 ÷ 5 = 600.

Now, suppose we select a sample of two individuals where x has measurements of 500 and 600. The sample average is (500 + 600) ÷ 2 = 1100 ÷ 2 = 550.

Here, the sampling error of the estimate = 600 (true value) – 550 (estimate) = 50.

Non-Sampling Errors

Non-sampling errors are more serious than sampling errors because a sampling error can be minimised by taking a larger sample. It is difficult to minimise non-sampling error, even by taking a large sample. Even a Census can contain non-sampling errors.

Errors in data acquisition

This type of error arises from recording of incorrect responses. Suppose the teacher asks the students to measure the length of the teacher's table in the classroom. The measurement by the students may differ. The differences may occur due to differences in measuring tape, carelessness of the students etc. Similarly, suppose we want to collect data on prices of oranges. We know that prices vary from shop to shop and from market to market. Prices also vary according to the quality. Therefore, we can only consider the average prices. Recording mistakes can also take place as the enumerators or the respondents may commit errors in recording or transcription the data, for example, he/ she may record 13 instead of 31.

Non-response errors

Non-response occurs if an interviewer is unable to contact a person listed in the sample or a person from the sample refuses to respond. In this case, the sample observation may not be representative.

Sampling bias

Sampling bias occurs when the sampling plan is such that some members of the target population could not possibly be included in the sample.

Sampling Error: an estimate of precision; estimates how close sample estimates are to a true population value for a characteristic. occurs as a result of selecting a sample rather than surveying an entire population

Standard Error: (SE) a measure of sampling error. Sampling Error is an inverse function of sample size. As sample size increases, SE decreases and sample become more precise. So, if we have smallest SE we may get greatest precision. If there is any doubt it is suggested to increase sample size.

Observer Effects

As methods have biases, so do observers. Bias is only one factor that contributes to observer error (Rosenthal 1976). Observer errors can contribute to a decrease in both reliability and validity; therefore the results are only as good as the observer.

Good data mean that they are an *accurate* measurement of the true situation. An observer may be *precise;* that is, his data will not vary greatly, but because of biases they might not be accurate. For example, consider two riflemen firing at two targets at a rifle range. Rifleman A groups his five shots closely (good precision) and in the bull's-eye (good accuracy). Rifleman B groups his five shots closely (good precision) but to the right of the bull's-eye (poor accuracy). Rifleman B's accuracy is biased by his always pulling his rifle slightly to the right while squeezing the trigger.

3.5. SUMMARY

- Facts, expressed in terms of numbers, are called data. The purpose of data collection is to understand, explain and analyse a problem and causes behind it. Primary data is obtained by conducting a survey.
- Survey includes various steps, which need to be planned carefully. There are various agencies which collect, process, tabulate and publish statistical data. These can be used as secondary data. However, the choice of source of data and mode of data collection depends on the objective of the study.
- Data is a tool which helps in reaching a sound conclusion on any problem by providing information.
- Primary data is based on first hand information.
- Survey can be done by personal interviews, mailing questionnaires and telephone interviews.
- Census covers every individual/unit belonging to the population.
- Sample is a smaller group selected from the population from which the relevant information would be sought.
- In a random sampling, every individual is given an equal chance of being selected for providing information.
- Sampling error arises due to the difference between the actual population and the estimate.
- Non-sampling errors can arise in data acquisition, by non-response or by bias in selection.

Chapter – 4

Sample Size Calculation

Studying this chapter will enable us:
- *To know how to estimate sample size for Population Proportion*
- *To know how to estimate sample size for Population Mean*
- *To know how to estimate sample size for testing equality of two Proportion*
- *To know how to estimate sample size for control study*
- *To know how to estimate sample size for comparing two Population Mean*

4.1. INTRODUCTION

The number of individuals to be included in a research study (the sample size of the study), is an important consideration in the design of many studies. This chapter will provide information on basic factors that determine an appropriate sample size and provides methods for its calculation in some simple, yet common, cases. Sample size is closely tied to statistical power, which is the ability of a study to enable detection of a statistically significant difference. A trade-off exists between a feasible sample size and adequate statistical power. Strategies for reducing the necessary sample size while maintaining a reasonable power is also important.

How many individuals will I need to study? This question is commonly asked by the clinical, ecological and behavioural investigator and exposes one of many issues that are best settled before actually carrying out a study. Consultation with a statistician is worthwhile in addressing many issues of study design, but a statistician is not always readily available.

The amount of information that can be gained from a sample depends upon its absolute size and not upon its size as a proportion of the population size, Just as to decide if the wine is good we need only a sip, irrespective of the bottle size, similarly we do not need to know the exact size of the parent population, provided complete homogeneity exists, But in reality, and more so in biological sciences, such homogeneity is rarely seen. Therefore, appropriate sample size becomes pertinent for drawing valid conclusions and is among the most difficult decisions to be taken for a study.

The size of the sample would depend upon (i) the *permissible error* in assessment of inference i.e. accuracy and (ii) *sampling error*. Sampling error measures the amount of variability between sample results; the lesser it is the better. The main determinant of the sample size, therefore, is how accurate results do we used. This in turn, depends on the purpose and type of study.

4.2. FOR DESCRIPTIVE STUDIES

In descriptive studies, generally, the objective is to obtain an estimate of the population parameter. For example, we may be interested to find the average caloric intake of the population or the proportion of people who are overweight, etc. Four aspects need to be known for determining the sample size:

- Identification of the 'characteristic of interest' viz. prevalence rate;
- 'Probability distribution' of the characteristic of interest viz. standard normal or binomial, etc;
- 'Sampling distribution' of several observed samples, as an indicator of inherent errors for extrapolating sample inferences to the population; and, most importantly; .
- 'Accuracy' i.e. how closely do we want our estimate to be matching the actual population value. A concise way of expressing this is through 'standard error'.

The calculation of sample size for descriptive studies, therefore, depends on the estimation of two parameters:

(i) Width of the confidence interval and
(ii) Confidence coefficient,

(Details discussed somewhere else).

Common situations of sample size calculation are:

For Estimating Population Proportion (p)

Suppose we want to conduct a study to find out the prevalence (P) of a relatively common disease in the community. We need to determine how many people should be observed to obtain a reasonably accurate picture of the prevalence. The following assumptions are necessary:

a. Confidence coefficient $(1 - \alpha)^*$: 95%
b. Width of the interval (δ) : 10%
c. Assumed prevalence** : 50% and
d. The condition is randomly distributed in a relatively large population.

* i.e. prevalence of condition would be within ±5% of true value or with 95% confidence.

** Assumed prevalence is based on prior information from other similar studies or, if that also is not available then, we use 50%, which will give the largest sample size.

Sample size, $n = (Z_1\text{-}\alpha/\delta)^2 \, p \, (1 - p)$
$= (1.96/5)^2 \, (50 \times 50)$
$= 385$

It means that at least 385 observations have to be made randomly in a population for estimating the prevalence (P) of a relatively common disease.

For Estimating Population Mean (μ)

Let us estimate the mean calorie intake of people in a community, assumed to have Gaussian distribution around mean μ, with a standard deviation, σ. The standard deviation, σ is either obtained from other similar studies or from a small number of observations through a pilot study. If either is not available, we can make a guess of the σ by dividing the range (maximum value - minimum value) by 4.

The following assumptions are necessary:

a. Confidence coefficient : 95%
b. Width of the interval : 50 cal
c. Standard deviation : 150 cal

95% confidence interval for sample mean will be

$$\bar{x} \pm Z_{(1-\alpha)} \sigma / \sqrt{n}$$

Or

$$n = \bar{x} \pm Z_{(1-\alpha)} \sigma^2$$

Then, sample size, $n = (1.96 \times 150/50)^2 = 35$ observations.

This sample size can also be used for analytical studies.

Computer programs are readily available, e.g. EPIINFO, for computation of sample sizes. They are specially warranted for complex situation, as required for estimation of Relative Risk (RR) or Odds Ratio (OR).

4.3. FOR ANALYTICAL STUDIES

The analytical study is generally used to test a null hypothesis. The determination of sample size, therefore, requires specifying the limits of error we are willing to accept while accepting or rejecting the null hypothesis (i.e. type I (α) and type II (β) errors). Apart from this, we have to determine the sample measures like a proportion/mean etc., as in the case of descriptive studies.

Type I error, or (α) is the probability of making a false conclusion that the two proportions are not equal in the population, when they are in fact equal. While type II error, or (β) is the probability of making a false decision that the two proportions are equal when they are really not i.e. 'null hypothesis is not true'. A simple way to decide that the 'null hypothesis is not true', is by defining the smallest difference (δ) is the two proportions which we consider clinically significant and calculate β under this hypothesis. Common situations of sample size calculation in analytic studies could be following:

For Testing Equality of Two Proportions ($\pi_1 = \pi_2$)

Sample size, $n = \left[\left\{ Z_{(n-a)} \sqrt{2\bar{\pi}(1-\bar{\pi})} - Z_\beta \sqrt{\pi_1(1-\pi_1) + \pi_2(1-\pi_2)} \right\} / \delta \right]^2$

Where $\bar{\pi} = \pi_1 + \pi_2 / 2$

For example, we may want to calculate sample size for the clinical trial of a new drug which improves survival among cancer patients. If the survival rate of patients given older drug is 40%, π_1 = 0.4. We want to check if new drug improves survival by at least 10% δ = 0.10 and hence It, = 0.50. If we want to restrict type I error at 5% then α = 0.05; therefore, $Z_{1-\alpha}$ = 1.96. We also want the type II error, β to be 5%, or we want to detect a difference of 10% or more with a probability of 95%, therefore, Z_β = - 1.645. Substituting these values, in above equation, we get n = 640. It means the study would require 640 subjects in each of the two groups, to assure a probability of detecting an increase in the survival rate of 10% or more with 95% certainty, if the statistical test used 5% as the level of significance.

For Case-Control Study

If we presume that long-term use of Oral Contraceptive Pill (OCP) increases the risk of Coronary Heart Disease (CHD), we are interested to know the sample size sufficient to detect an increase in relative risk (actually OR) of ≥ 30% by means of a case-control study. The hypothesis can be stated as the proportion of women using (OCPs) is the same among those with CHD and those without CHD'. Let us suppose, 20% women without CHD use OCPs (control). Then, since we have decided the need to detect an OR ≥ 1.3, the use of OCPs among women with CHD must be 20 + .3 x 20 = 26%. Choosing α and β to be 5% each, the sample size, using the above formula comes to 2220. This means that we need to study 2220 cases and 2220 controls.

For Comparing Two Population Means

When a study involves comparing the means of two samples, the sample measure used is the difference of the sample means. In the simplest scenario,

the sample size, $n = (Z_{1-\alpha} - Z_\beta)\sigma / \delta^2$

Let us suppose we want to test a drug that reduces blood pressure. We want to say the drug is effective if the reduction in BP is ≥ 5 mm of Hg, as compared to a placebo. If the systolic BP in the population has Gaussian distriution with standard deviation of 8 mm Hg, α is chosen at 0.05 and β also at 0.05, then the sample size required for this study would be,

$n = [(1.96 + 1.645) \times 8 / 3]^2$
$= 34$

That is there should be 34 subjects in each group.

For Comparing More Than Two Groups (multivariate methods)

The formula used for arriving at the sample size in these situations is quite complex and hence is not being discussed here.

4.4. SURVEY / SAMPLING IN ECOLOGY

Generally, following two methods are used to study the ecology:

A. Non-Sampling Method

a. Total count in an area

   e.g. Siberian cranes in Keoladeo national park, Rajasthan

b. Nest count

   e.g. Greater Adjutant stork colony

c. Territory mapping

   e.g. Bengal florican display grounds

B. Sampling Strategy

- Counting a small representative population and then extrapolating about the total population

   e.g. random, stratified or systematic random

Important Points to Remember -

- Do not unnecessary collect large data
- Maximize your efforts
- Determine sample size
- Collect right type of data

To determine effective sampling efforts, first answer two major questions:

1. How many samples to take?
2. What should be the plot size so that most species are covered?

To answer these questions:

We need to plot *Species Discovery Curve*.

Sample Size Calculation

Species Discovery Curve is plotting of number of species detected or discovered per unit of sampling efforts (length of transect, time spent on walking a transect or standing on a point).

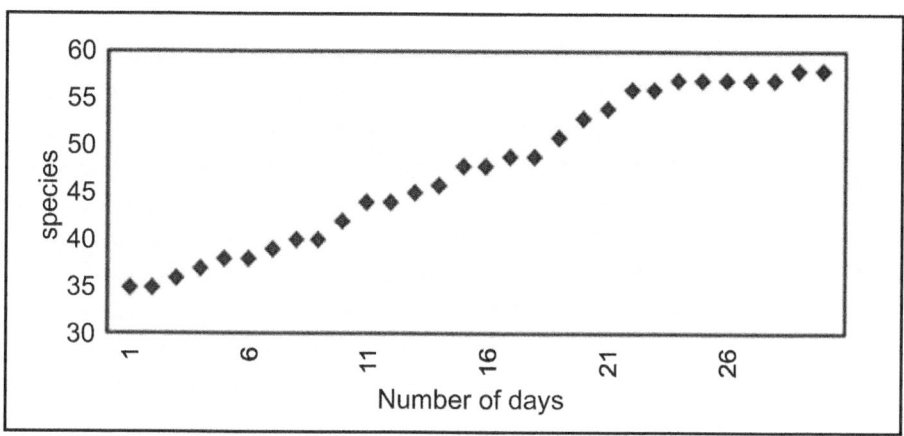

Courtesy Javed and Kaul 2001

Fig : Species discovery curve per unit days

4.5. SUMMARY

Sample size depends on
- Permissible error
- Variability between samples

Optimum sample size for
- Estimating *population proportion (P)* for descriptive study

  $n = (Z_1 - \alpha/\delta)^2 \, p \, (1 - p) = 385$ at 95% confidence level

- Estimating (or comparing) *population mean* (u) for any study type

  $n = \bar{x} \pm Z_{(1-\alpha)} \sigma / \sqrt{n} = 35$ at 95% confidence level

- Testing equality of *proportions* (7t. = 7t2) for analytical study

  $n = \left[\left\{ Z_{(1-\alpha)} \sqrt{2\bar{\pi}_1(1-\bar{\pi})} - Z_\beta \sqrt{\pi_1(1-\pi_1) + \pi_2(1-\pi_2)} \right\} / \delta \right]^2$

  = 640 for each group (at 95% confidence levels)

Estimating optimal sample size for ecological study
- Draw species discovery curve

Chapter – 5

Concept of Probability

Studying this chapter will enable us:
- *To Quantify the chance*
- *To know what will be the possible outcome from a single trial*
- *To know what will be probability if an event is certain to happen*
- *To know what will be probability if an event is certain not to happen?*

5.1. INTRODUCTION

The word 'probability' means "reasonable likelihood of happening of an event". In biology it is difficult to predict an outcome with absolute certainty. Probability helps us to estimate the occurrence of relative frequency of any (biological) event and is an accepted *measure of uncertainty*.

Mathematically, the probability 'P' that an event 'E' will occur, is expressed as:

$$P(E) = \frac{\text{number of times E occurs}}{\text{number of times E can occur}}$$

Therefore, it is logical that the probability value should be between 0 and 1. Zero (0) means the event cannot occur and 1 means the event will definitely occur. A value of 0.5 means the probability that the event will occur is the same as the probability that it will not occur. The sum of the probabilities i.e. relative frequencies of all events that can occur in the sample should be 1 or 100%.

5.2. FOR SINGLE EVENTS

Unconditional Probability

Biological events can be simple phenomenon like survival or death and when these are assumed to be unrelated to other events, the estimation of probability becomes relatively simple and can be done with the simple formula mentioned above. This is called *unconditional probability*.

For example, the chances of survival after rabies are zero and that after uncomplicated acute respiratory infection is 100%. Or, if a surgeon transplants kidney in 200 cases and patient survives in 80 cases, then the probability of survival,

$$P(E) = \frac{\text{number of times E occurs}}{\text{number of times E can occur}}$$

$$P(E) = \frac{80}{200}$$

The probability of survival is 40%, and is called unconditional because, it has been computed without knowing whether another event has occurred.

Note that the denominator of unconditional probability is the total number of patients studied.

However, in contrast to above, more commonly, we have to deal with two or more events, which may or may not have some form of mutual relationship.

5.3. INDEPENDENT EVENTS

Mutually Exclusive Relationship

This means the occurrence of one event excludes the probability of occurrence of another event; i.e. these events can't occur at the same time. For example, the birth of a male child excludes the probability of birth of a female or neuter gender child (in this birth). Or having blood group A, excludes the possibility of having any of the other three groups viz. B, 0, or AB.

Mutually exclusive events follow the *additive law of probability*, according to which,

$$P(A \text{ or } B) = P(A) + P(B)$$

Not Mutually Exclusive "Relationship

Events that are not mutually exclusive can consist of union of two events A and B. In other words, it will contain all the elements belonging *either* to event A *or* to event B. For example, being a male and having a particular blood group, say A, are independent events that have a not mutually exclusive relationship. Mathematically, it is denoted as P(A or B) using a modification of the previously referred addition rule.

$$P(A \text{ or } B) = P(A) + P(B) - P(A \text{ and } B)$$

Note that the overlap of the two events is denoted as P(A and B).

Occurring Simultaneously

Two events are said to be *independent* if the probability of one does not affect the probability of the other. If the events are independent, the probability that A and B occurs jointly is denoted by the *multiplication rule* of probability. Mathematically, it is denoted as,

$$P(A \text{ and } B) = P(A) P(B)$$

Note that it is actually the intersection of the two probabilities.

5.4. NOT INDEPENDENT EVENTS

Occurring Jointly (Joint Probability)

There can be instances when elements can have experience of both events A as well as B. Suppose we are studying Down's syndrome and mental retardation. The joint probability here will represent the simultaneous occurrence (i.e. intersection) of both the events that is a child having Down's syndrome and also mentally retarded.

Mathematically, it is denoted as,

$$P(A \text{ and } B) = P(A|B) P(B)$$

Occurring Conditionally (Conditional Probability)

If the probability of occurrence of one event increases or decreases the probability of the other event, then the two events are said to be not independent, or dependent. The probability estimated in such conditions is called conditional probability, meaning that our focus is on the occurrence of an event given that another outcome has already occurred. The conditional probability of A, given B, is the joint probability divided by the probability of B. Mathematically, it is denoted as P(AIB), where the vertical line is read as 'given' (probability of A given B).

$$P(AIB) = \frac{P(A \text{ and } B)}{P(B)}$$

Where, $P(B) \neq 0$

Note that there is only a subtle difference between joint and conditional probability for not-independent events.

Significance of Probability

Probability provides the basis for all the tests of significance. The probability values in a population are distributed in a definable manner and this property is used to estimate whether a person selected randomly, from say 100 study participants, actually has the disease being investigated.

It is worthwhile to recall that the values of biological parameters follow typical distribution patterns in populations, viz. Gaussian, Binomial, Chi-square, etc., and *based on that knowledge* as well as 'probability' we apply a suitable *test of significance*.

Example: An outbreak of food poisoning occurred among the hostel inmates of a college. Custard served after dinner was suspected to be the carrier for the causative organisms. Epidemiological investigations revealed the following:

Custard	Food poisoning symptom		
	Present	Absent	Total
Consumed	90	30	120
Not consumed	20	60	80
Total	110	90	200

Compute the following probabilities:

(i) What is the probability of a hostel inmate becoming ill?

This is an example of *unconditional probability* and using formula

We get $P_{(FP)} = 110/200 = 0.55$.

(ii) What is the probability of hostel inmate consuming custard?

Like in above, $P_{(CC)} = 120/200 = 0.6$

(Unconditional probability)

(iii) What is the probability that an inmate becomes ill after consuming custard?

Here we have to find conditional probability

$$P_{(FP/CC)} = \frac{P_{(FP \text{ and } CC)}}{P_{(CC)}} = \frac{90/200}{120/200}$$

$$= 1.125$$

(iv) What is the probability that a student becomes ill without consuming custard?

Here also, as in (iii) we compute conditional probability using formula above mentioned.

$$P_{(FP/CC)} = \frac{P_{(FP \text{ and } CC)}}{P_{(CC)}} = \frac{20/200}{80/200} = 0.25$$

(v) What is the probability that an inmate falling ill consumed custard?

Using formula mentioned above for conditional probability again, we get,

$$= \frac{P_{(CC \text{ and } FP)}}{P_{(FP)}} = \frac{90/200}{110/200}$$

$$= 0.82$$

Note that the probability of becoming ill after consuming custard *(iii)* is not the same as probability of ill person consuming custard (v).

(vi) What is the probability of student eating custard and also falling sick supposing these are independent events?

The word 'and' denotes *'occurring together'* for independent events. Therefore, we use the multiplication rule of probability.

$$P_{(FP \text{ and } CC)} = P_{(FP)} P_{(CC)} =$$
$$= 110/200 \times 120/200$$
$$= 0.33$$

(vii) What is the probability that a student falls ill or eats custard? (Supposing these are independent events).

The word 'or' denotes that we have to use the *modified additive* rule.

$$P_{(A \text{ or } B)} = P_{(A)} + P_{(B)} - P_{(A \text{ and } B)}$$
$$= 0.55 + 0.6 - 0.33$$
$$= 0.82$$

(viii) What is the ratio of probabilities obtained for *(iii)* and *(iv)*? And what is its interpretation?

$$= \frac{P_{(FP/CC)}}{P_{(FP/CC-1)}} = \frac{0.75}{0.25} = 3$$

This means that an inmate who consumed custard is 3 times more likely to be ill as compared to one who did not consume custard.

5.5. SUMMARY

Probability for Single Events

- *Unconditional Probability*

$$P(E) = \frac{\text{number of times E occurs}}{\text{number of times E can occur}}$$

Probability for Independent Events

- *Mutually Exclusive Relationship*

  P(A or B) = P(A) + P(B)

- *Probability for Not Mutually Exclusive "Relationship*

  P(A or B) = P(A) + P{B) - P(A and B)

Note that the overlap of the two events is denoted as P(A and B).

- Probability for *Occurring Simultaneously*

  P(A and B) = P(A) P(B)

Note that it is actually the intersection of the two probabilities.

Probability for Not Independent Events

- *Occurring Jointly (Joint Probability)*

  P(A and B) = P(AIB) P(B)

- *Occurring Conditionally (Conditional Probability)*

$$P(AIB) = \frac{P(A \text{ and } B)}{P(B)}$$

Chapter – 6

Hypothesis Formulation

Studying this chapter will enable us:
- *To know the concept of hypothesis and its formulation*
- *To know the critical region, Significance level and Critical value*
- *To know one-tailed and two-tailed Tests*
- *To know how to decide Criterion for accepting or rejecting the hypothesis*
- *To know what is Type I and Type II Error*

6.1. INTRODUCTION

The word hypothesis is made up of two words *Hypo + thesis = Hypothesis*. 'Hypo' means tentative or subject to the verification and 'Thesis' means statement about solution of a problem.

The world meaning of the term hypothesis is a tentative statement about the solution of the problem. Hypothesis offers a solution of the problem that is to be verified empirically and based on some rationale. Hypothesis is the composition of some variables which have some specific position or role of the variables i.e. to be verified empirically. It is a proposition about the factual and conceptual elements. Hypothesis is called a leap into the dark. It is a brilliant guess about the solution of a problem. A tentative generalization or theory formulated about the character of phenomena under observation are called hypothesis. It is a statement temporarily accepted as true in the light of what is known at the time about the phenomena. It is the basis for planning and action in the research for new truth.

6.2. DEFINITIONS OF HYPOTHESIS

The term hypothesis has been defined in several ways. Some important definitions have been given in the following paragraphs:

I. According to *"James E. Greighton"* - A hypothesis is a tentative supposition or provisional guess ". It is a tentative supposition or provisional guess which seems to explain the situation under observation".

II. According to *Lungberg* - "A hypothesis is a tentative generalization the validity of which remains to be tested. In its most elementary stage the hypothesis may be any hunch, guess, imaginative idea which becomes the basis for further investigation."

III. According to *John W. Best* - "It is a shrewd guess or inference that is formulated and provisionally adopted to explain observed facts or conditions and to guide in further investigation."

IV. According to *A.D. Carmichael* - "Science employs hypothesis in guiding the thinking process. When our experience tells us that a given phenomenon follows regularly upon the appearance of certain other phenomena, we conclude that the former is connected with the latter by some sort of relationship and we form an hypothesis concerning this relationship".

V. According to *Goode and Han* - "A hypothesis states what we are looking for. A hypothesis looks forward. It is a proposition which can be put to a test to determine its validity. It may prove to be correct or incorrect.

VI. *Bruce W. Tuckman* stated that "A hypothesis then could be defined as an expectation about events based on generalization of the assumed relationship between variables."

VII. "A hypothesis is a tentative statement of the relationship between two or more variables. Hypotheses are always in declarative sentence form and they relate, either generally or specifically variable and variables."

VIII. According to *M. Verma* - "A theory when stated as a testable proposition formally and clearly and subjected to empirical or experimental verification is known as a hypothesis."

IX. *Barr and Scates* define hypothesis as a statement temporarily accepted as true in the light of what is, at the time, known about a phenomena, and it is employed as a basis for action in the search for new truth, when the hypothesis is fully established, it may take the form of facts, principles and theories."

X. Hypothesis is a testable proposition or assumption whose testability is to be tested on the basis of the computability of its implications with empirical evidence with previous knowledge."- *George, J. Mouly.*

Assumption, Postulate and Hypothesis

The terms assumption, postulate and hypothesis occur most frequently in the research literature, but are often confused by research scholars. Hence these terms need clear explanation.

(a) **Assumption:** Assumption means taking things for granted so that the situation is simplified for logical procedure. They facilitate the progress of an agreement by introducing restrictive conditions. For example, the formulas of Statistics and measurement are based on number of assumptions. Assumption means restrictive conditions before the argument can become valid. Assumptions are made on the basis of logical insight and their truthfulness can be observed on the basis of data or evidences.

(b) **Postulate**: Postulates are the working beliefs of most scientific activity. The mathematician begins by postulating a system of numbers which range from 0 to 9 and can permute and combine only thereafter. With many people God and Spirit is a postulate of the good life or godly life. Postulates are not proven; they are simply accepted at their face value so that their basic work for the discovery of other facts of nature can begin.

(c) **Hypothesis**: A hypothesis is different from both of these. It is the presumptive statement of a proposition which the investigator seeks to prove. It is a condensed generalization. This generalization requires knowledge of principles of things or essential characteristics which pertain to entire class of phenomena.

The hypothesis furnishes the germinal basis of the whole investigation and remains to test it out by facts. The hypothesis is based on some earlier theory and some rationale whereas postulates are taken as granted true. An assumption is the assumed solution of a major problem. It may be partially true. The scientific research process is based on some hypotheses. The natural sciences and mathematics are based on postulates. The statistic is based on some assumptions which are considered approximate science. The assumptions are helpful in conducting a research work in behavioural sciences.

Observation versus Specific and General Hypothesis

Hypotheses are often confused with observation. These terms refer to quite different things. An observation refers to; what is seen. From observation researcher may infer. For example a researcher may go into a school and after looking around observe that most of the students are dark faced. From that observation he may infer that the school is located in a poor neighbor-hood. Though the researcher does not know that the neighbor-hood is poor, he expects that the majority of people living there are poor. Then he has formulated a specific hypothesis setting forth an anticipated relationship between two variables like race and income level. For the test of this hypothesis researcher could walk around the neighbor-hood, observes the home and the income levels. After observation he provides support for this specific hypothesis and for this researcher might make a general hypothesis. The second hypothesis represents a generalization and must be tested by making observation as was the specific hypothesis. Since it would be impossible to observe all universe or population, thus the researchers will take a sample and reach conclusion on a probability basis for the verification of hypothesis being true or not. There is some difference between specific and general hypothesis. Specific hypothesis requires fewer observations for testing than the general hypothesis. For testing purpose a general hypothesis is reformulated to a more specific one.

Functions of Hypothesis

The following are the main functions of hypothesis in the research process suggested by H.H. Mc.Ashan:

1. It is a temporary solution of a problem concerning with some truth which enables an investigator to start his research works.
2. It offers a basis in establishing the specifics what to study for and may provide possible solutions to the problem.
3. Each hypothesis may lead to formulate another hypothesis.
4. A preliminary hypothesis may take the shape of final hypothesis.
5. Each hypothesis provides the investigator with definite statement which may be objectively tested and accepted or rejected and leads for interpreting results and drawing conclusions that is related to original purpose.

The functions of a hypothesis may be condensed into three. The following are the threefold functions of a hypothesis:

(a) To delimit the field of the investigation.
(b) To sensitize the researcher so that he should work selectively, and have very realistic approach to the problem.
(c) To offer the simple means for collecting evidences to the verification.

Importance of a Hypothesis

I. "Carter V. Good" thinks that hypothesis works as Investigator's *"Eyes"*. Hypothesis guides the investigator in further investigation it serves as the investigator's "Eyes" in seeking answers to tentatively adopted generalization.

II. Hypothesis Focuses Research. Without it, research is unfocussed research and remains like a random empirical wandering. It serves as necessary link between theory and the investigation.

III. Hypothesis Places Clear and Specific Goals. A well thought out set of hypothesis is that they place clear and specific goals before the research worker and provide him with a basis for selecting sample and research procedure to meet these goals.

IV. *"Good Barr and Scates"* suggest that Hypothesis Links Together. It serves the important function of linking together related facts and information and organizing them into wholes.

V. "*P. V. Young*" considers that hypothesis prevents scientists from Blind Research. The use of hypothesis prevents a blind search and indiscriminate gathering of masses of data which may later prove irrelevant to the problem under study.

VI. A hypothesis serves as a powerful inspiration those lights the way for the research work.

VII. George J. Mouley thinks that Hypotheses serve the following purposes:

1. They provide direction to research and prevent the review of irrelevant literature and the collection of excess data.

2. They sensitize the investigator certain aspects of situation which are irrelevant from the standpoint of the problem at hand.

3. They enable the investigator to understand with greater clarity his problem and its consequence.

4. They serve as a framework for the conclusive-in short a good hypothesis:

    (a) Gives help in deciding the direction in which he has to proceed.

    (b) It helps in selecting significant fact.

    (c) It helps in drawing conclusions.

VIII. D.B. Van Dalen advocates the Importance of Hypothesis in the following ways:

1. Hypotheses are indispensable research instrument, for they build a bridge between the problem and the location of empirical evidence that may solve the problem.

2. A hypothesis provides the map that guides and expedites the exploration of the phenomena under consideration.

3. A hypothesis pin points the problem. The investigator can examine thoroughly the factual and conceptual elements that appear to be related to a problem.

Hypothesis Formulation

4. Using hypothesis determines the relevancy of facts. A hypothesis directs the researcher's efforts into productive channels.

5. The hypothesis indicates not only what to look for is an investigation but how to obtain data. It helps in deciding research design. It may suggest what subjects, tests, tools, and techniques are needed.

6. The hypothesis provides the investigator with the most efficient instrument for exploring and explaining the unknown facts.

7. A hypothesis provides the framework for drawing conclusions.

8. These hypotheses simulate the investigator for further research studies.

IX. Bruce W. Tuckman presents the importance of Hypothesis in the Research Spectrum:

1. Research begins with a problem and utilization of both theories and findings in arriving at hypothesis.

2. These hypotheses contain variables which must be labeled and then operationally defined to construct predictions. These steps might be considered the logical stages of the research. These stages are followed by methodological stages, which culminate in the development of research design and development of measures and finally in the finding themselves.

The Role of Hypotheses

The hypotheses play following significant role in the scientific studies:

a) The purpose of stating hypothesis is to provide a framework for the research procedure and methodology. It directs the research activities.

b) A research project needs to proceed from a statement of hypotheses. Such hypotheses aids to the research process.

c) A hypothesis takes on some characteristics of a theory which is usually considered as a larger set of generalization about a certain phenomenon.

d) The verification of a hypothesis does not prove or disprove it; it merely sustains or refutes the hypotheses.

e) The hypotheses may imply research procedures to be used and necessary data to be organized. Such hypotheses are not ends in themselves but rather aids to the research process.

f) The stating a hypothesis in experimental research provide the basis for designing the experiment and collecting evidences empirically for its verification so as to formulate new theory.

Limitations of Hypotheses

The following objections are raised against stating hypotheses which are directional in nature:

I. Hypotheses bias the researcher in favour of certain conclusions or retain the hypotheses.

II. While stating the hypothesis, researcher may overlook other possibly worthwhile hypotheses.

III. The statement of hypotheses in some situations also may appear premature.

IV. The researcher may decide to defer any hypothesis or theories until he has some empirical evidence.

V. The hypotheses are stated in vacuum. These should be concerned with a situation in which it can be experienced.

VI. The directional hypotheses should be so stated as to reveal the role of variables involved in the investigation.

VII. The hypothesis orients the research process for its verification but does not help in finding out the solution of the problem.

6.3. TYPES OF HYPOTHESES

1. Null Hypothesis
2. Alternate Hypothesis

(1) Null Hypothesis

Null hypothesis is most usual hypothesis and symbolized as H_O. This means "the hypothesis of no difference". It is called null hypothesis because it 'nullifies' the positive argument of the findings.

Null hypothesis may be stated in the null form which is an assertion that no relationship or no difference exists between or among

Hypothesis Formulation

the variables. It assumes that no or zero difference exists between the two population means or the treatments. This type of hypothesis is also termed as statistical hypothesis or non-directional hypothesis or zero hypothesis because it denies the existence of any systematic principles apart from the effect of chance.

Suppose we want to see relationship between human population and number of bank branches in a city.

In this case Null hypothesis (Ho) would be: Population do not have any influence on the number of bank branches in a town.

(2) Alternate Hypothesis

Any null hypothesis must have alternative – usually designated as H_1. An alternate hypothesis is formulated when a researcher totally rejects null hypothesis.

As above if we want to see relationship between human population and number of bank branches in a city.

Aternate hypothesis (H_1) would be: Population has significant effect on the number of bank branches in a town.

Test Statistics and Statistical Significance

The objective of each of the statistical test is to produce single number called a "test statistic". The important feature of a test static is that its probability distribution is known (its value is already calculated by statistician) and denoted by "z"

6.4. DIVISIONS OF NORMAL DISTRIBUTION CURVE WITH

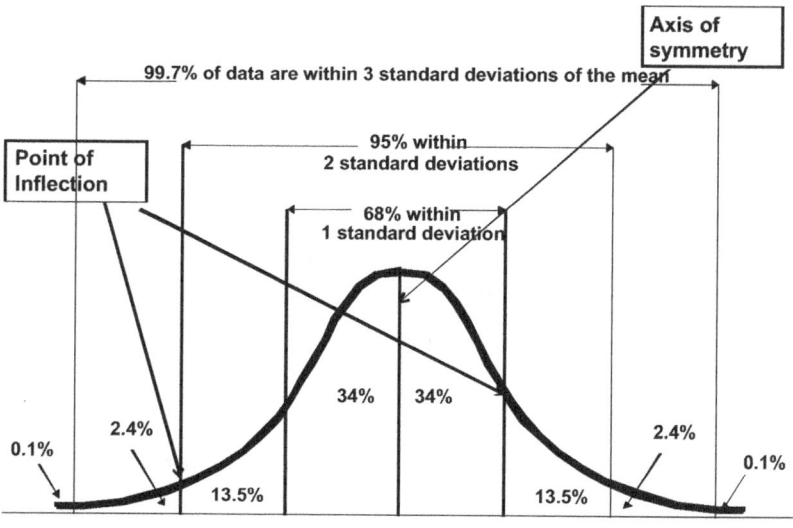

The curve shown above is an example of a standard normal distribution which has great importance in statistics.

If we consider total area under normal distribution curve equal to 100%, then 68% of the total area will fall within 1 standard deviation on either side of mean (i.e. ±1 SD) as shown in above figure.

By extending the limits to 2 standard deviation units (z = ± 2), the proportion of observations will increase and area cover will be 95.44% and similarly, 99.74% of observation will fall within ± 3SD (z = ±3). These levels of probability are converted to 95% and 99% by applying an appropriate correction.

Thus,

68% of all observation fall within ± 1 SD (z = ± 1)

95% of all observations fall within ± 1.96 SD (z = ± 1.96)

99% of all observations fall within ± 2.58 SD (z = ± 2.58)

The probability that an observation selected at random from the sample will fall outside ± 1.96 SD is $p = 0.05$, and outside ± 2.58 SD is $p = 0.01$. If the probability of an observation falling outside a z value of ± 1.96 is less than $p = 0.05$, such an observation is therefore considered "significant".

In each case, a statistical test produces a value for its test statistic, and the task is to determine whether that value exceeds some probability threshold, if so, the null hypothesis will be rejected.

6.5. DECISION CRITERION FOR ACCEPTING OR REJECTING THE HYPOTHESIS

Traditional Method

Reject H_0 if the test statistic falls within the critical region.

Fail to *reject H_0* if the test statistic does not fall within the critical region.

P-value method

The *P*-value (or probability value) is the probability of getting a value of the test statistic that is *at least as extreme* as the one representing the sample data, assuming that the null hypothesis is true.

Reject H_0 if P-value ≤ α (where α is the significance level, such as 0.05).

Fail to *reject H_0* if P-value > α.

The different levels of significance are often expressed as follows:

*	= p <00.05 (5% level)	significant
**	= p<0.01 (1% level)	highly significant
***	= p<0.001 (0.1 level)	very highly significant

Another option

Instead of using a significance level such as 0.05, simply identify the P-value and leave the decision to the reader.

The critical region

The critical region (or rejection region) is the set of all values of the test statistic that cause us to reject the null hypothesis.

For example, see the dark-shaded region.

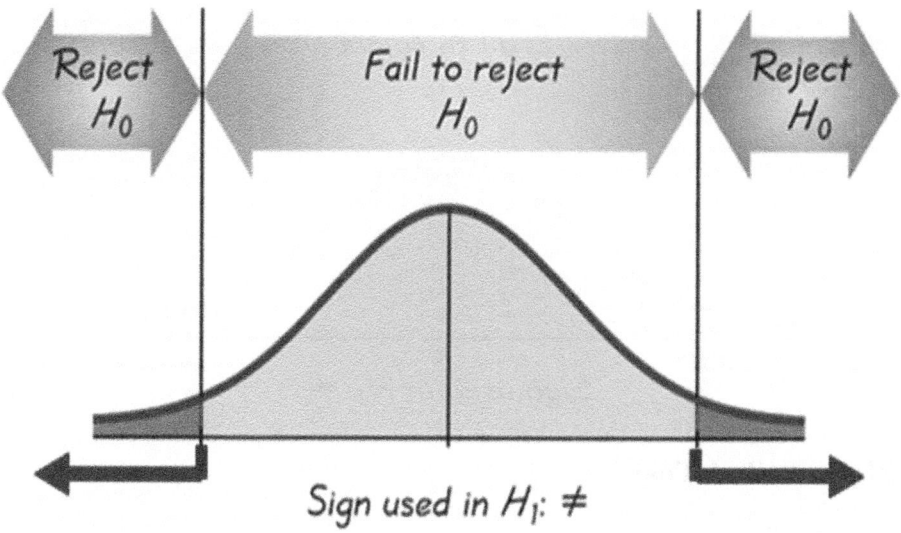

Significance level

The significance level (denoted by) is the probability that the test statistic will fall in the critical region when the null hypothesis is actually true.

Common choices for α are 0.05, 0.01, and 0.00.1.

Critical Value

A critical value is any value separating the critical region (where we reject the H_0) from the values of the test statistic that does not lead to rejection of the null hypothesis, the sampling distribution that applies, and the significance level α.

For example, the critical value of $z = 1.645$ corresponds to a significance level of $\alpha = 0.05$.

6.6. TWO-TAILED TESTS

The tails in a distribution are the extreme regions bounded by critical values.

Two-Tailed Test

H_0: =
H_1: ≠

Here, α is divided equally between the two tails of the critical region

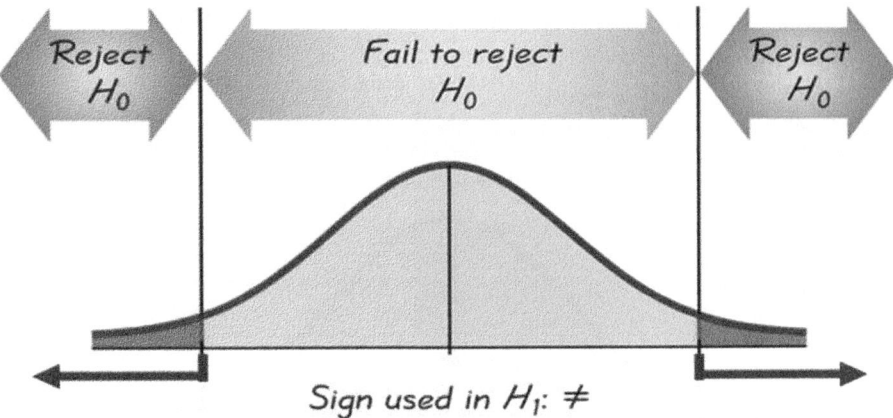

Right-Tailed Test

H_0: =
H_1: >

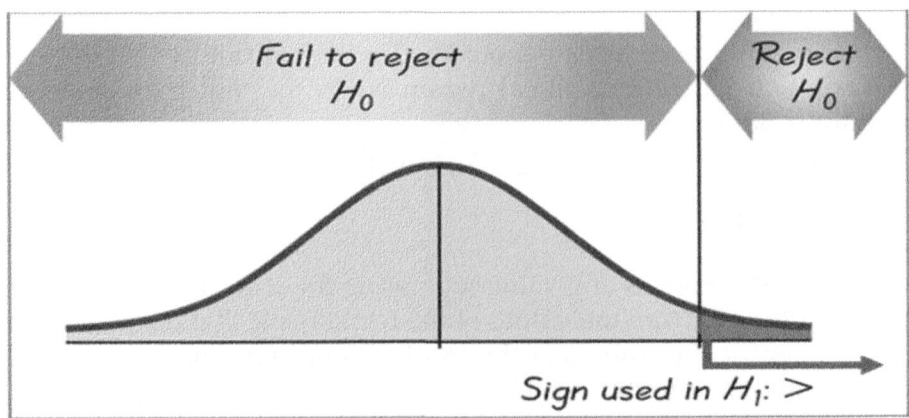

Left-Tailed Test

H_0: =
H_1: <

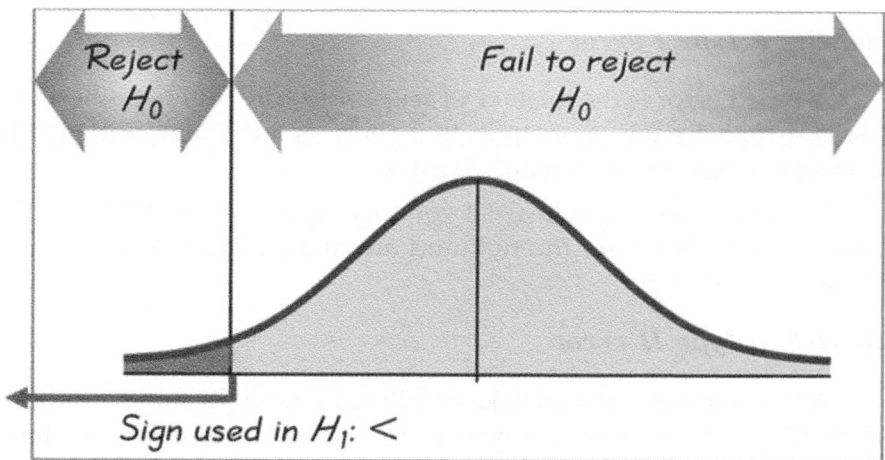

6.7. TYPES OF ERRORS

There are two types of Errors:

Type I Error

A Type I error is the mistake of rejecting the null hypothesis when it is true.

The symbol α (alpha) is used to represent the probability of a type I error.

Type II Error

A Type II error is the mistake of failing to reject the null hypothesis when it is false.

The symbol β (beta) is used to represent the probability of a type II error.

Example: Assume that we are conducting a hypothesis test of the claim $p > 0.5$. Here are the null and alternative hypotheses: H_0: $p = 0.5$, and H_1: $p > 0.5$.

a)   Identify a type I error.
b)   Identify a type II error.

Example: Assume that we are conducting a hypothesis test of the claim $p > 0.5$.

Here, null and alternative hypotheses are: $H_0: p = 0.5$, and $H_1: p > 0.5$.

Identify a type I error

A type I error is the mistake of rejecting a true null hypothesis, so this is a type I error: Conclude that there is sufficient evidence to support $p > 0.5$, when in reality $p = 0.5$.

Example: Assume that we a conducting a hypothesis test of the claim $p > 0.5$. Here are the null and alternative hypotheses: $H_0: p = 0.5$, and $H_1: p > 0.5$.

Identify a type II error

A type II error is the mistake of failing to reject the null hypothesis when it is false, so this is a type II error: Fail to reject $p = 0.5$ (and therefore fail to support $p > 0.5$) when in reality $p > 0.5$.

Type I and Type II Errors

		The Null Hypothesis is true	The Null Hypothesis is false
Decision	We decide to reject the null hypothesis	**Type I Error** (rejecting a true null hypothesis) α	Correct decision
	We fail to reject the null hypothesis	Correct decision	**Type II Error** (failing to reject a false null hypothesis) β

Controlling Type I and Type II Errors

For any fixed α, an increase in the sample size n will cause a decrease in β.

For any fixed sample size n, a decrease in α, will cause an increase in β. Conversely, an increase in α, will cause a decrease in β.

To decrease both α and β, increase the sample size.

Power of a Hypothesis Test

The power of a hypothesis test is the probability $(1 - \beta)$ of rejecting a false null hypothesis, which is computed by using a particular

Hypothesis Formulation

significance level α and a particular value of the population parameter that is an alternative to the value assumed true in the null hypothesis.

Trade-Off in Probability for Two Errors

There is an inverse relationship between the probabilities of the two types of errors.

Increase probability of a type 1 error => decrease in probability of a type 2 error

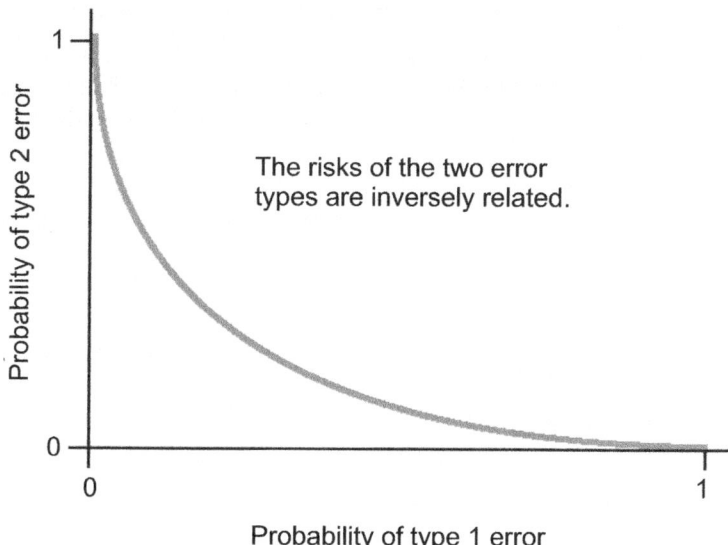

General relationship between the probabilities of two errors

Type 2 Errors and Power

There are three factors that affect probability of a type 2 error

a) Sample size; larger n reduces the probability of a type 2 error without affecting the probability of a type 1 error.

b) Level of significance; larger α reduces probability of a type 2 error by increasing the probability of a type 1 error.

c) Actual value of the population parameter;

When the alternative hypothesis is true, the probability of making the correct decision is called the power of a test.

Example

Imagine that the goal is to test H_0: μ ≤ 15 assuming normality, σ=4, and that the Type I error probability is to be .01. Then $1-\alpha$ = .99

and from table (in appendix) $c = 2.33$. If based on a sample of size 25, the sample mean is $\bar{X} = 18$, we have that

$$Z = \frac{\frac{18-15}{4}}{\sqrt{25}}$$

$$= 3.75$$

Because 3.75 is greater than 2.33, reject the null hypothesis.

We repeat example given above, only now we test $H_0: \mu = 15$, again assuming normality, $\sigma = 4$, and that the Type I error probability is to be .01. So $\alpha/2 = 0.005$, $1-\alpha/2 = 0.995$, and from table in appendix, $c = 2.58$. Because $|Z| = 3.75 > 2.58$, reject the null hypothesis.

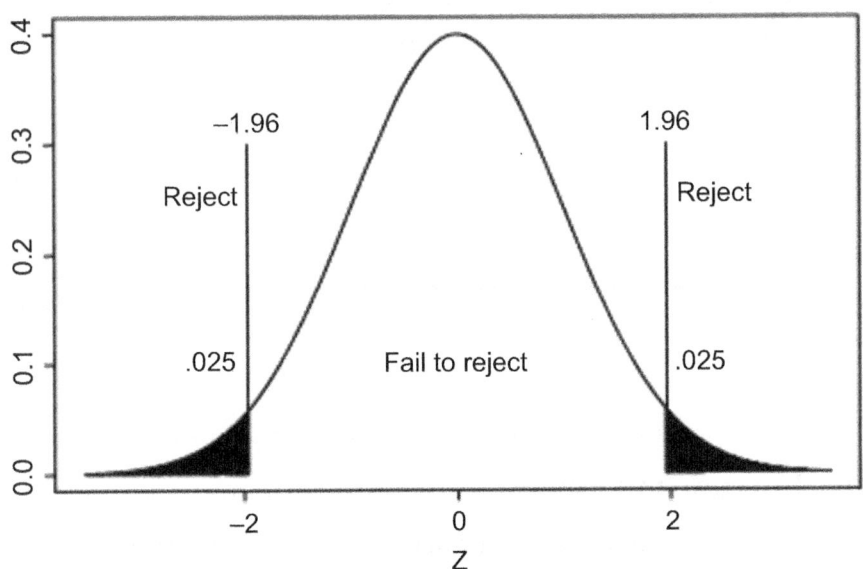

A graphical depiction of the rejection rule when using Z and $\alpha = .05$. The shaded portions indicate the rejection regions.

Hypothesis Formulation

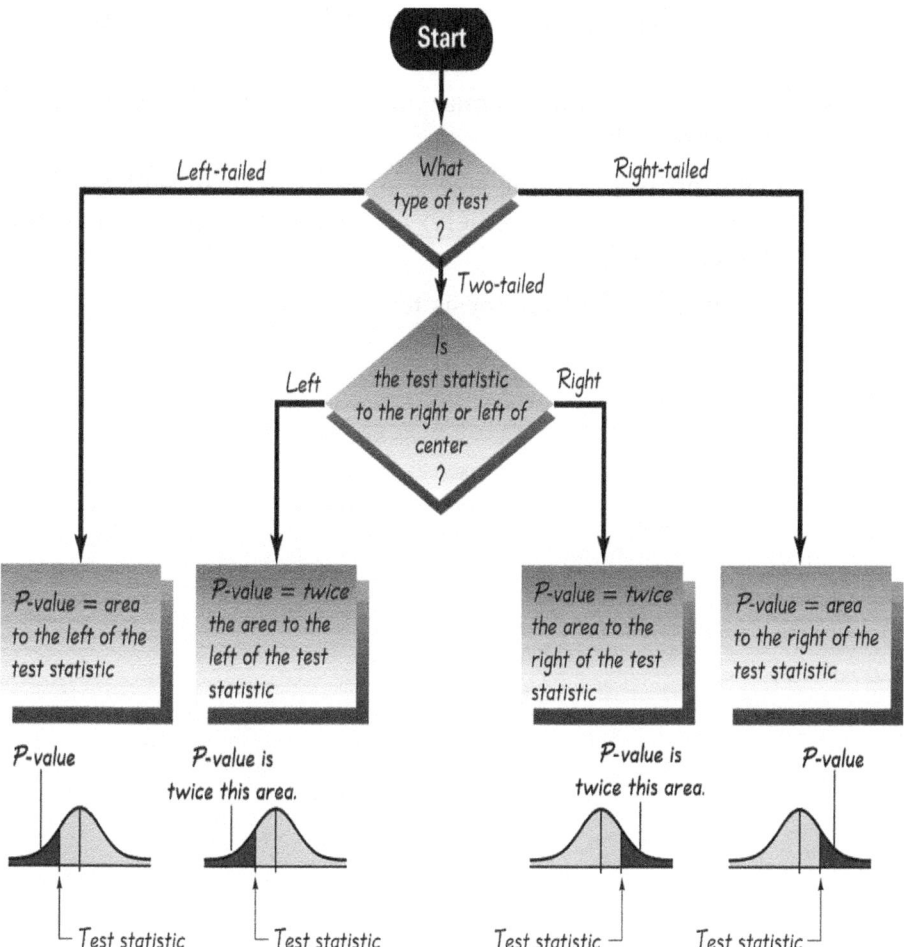

6.8. SUMMARY

Definitions of Hypothesis
- A hypothesis is a tentative supposition or provisional guess.
- It is a tentative supposition or provisional guess which seems to explain the situation under observation.

Identification of Type I and Type II error
- A type I error is the mistake of rejecting a true null hypothesis.
- A type II error is the mistake of failing to reject the null hypothesis when it is false.

Controlling Type I, Type II Errors and Power of a Hypothesis Test

- For any fixed α, an increase in the sample size n will cause a decrease in β.
- For any fixed sample size n, a decrease in α, will cause an increase in β. Conversely, an increase in α, will cause a decrease in β.
- The power of a hypothesis test is $(1 - \beta)$.

Chapter – 7

How to Write Research Proposal

Studying this chapter will enable us:
- *To know the concept of Research Proposal*
- *To know what are the basic pre-requisite to develop a good Research Proposal*
- *To know writing a good Research/Project proposal that may help in planning research*

1.1. INTRODUCTION

Researchers interested in taking up research have initial difficultes in picking up a problem worth for investigation. At time they waste considerable amount of time in just thinking about the pros and cons of problems suggested by some ones or identified by himself/herself. It is basically due to misunderstanding about "what is research". Usual notion about research is that it must resuit in something spectacular or it must come up with a new discovery or theory. It must be pointed out that a study which brings forward new facts, or which demolishes or establishes a hypothesis or a theory or principal already in vogue, or which puts a variety of information in to order or system, or which prepares ground for further research is as valid as one which ends with a new discovery. The best research problem for researcher is one which arises from the researcher's own curiosity. The only thing is that researcher must know the tools which can handle the problems he proposed to take up. Before choosing for a problem for research one should as question to himself: is this problem really of interest to me?; Is it significant in the sense that it extends the frontiers of knowledge or fills an important gap in knowledge?; Can I handle this problem within the constraints of resources of money, time etc?; has this problem not been investigated by someone else? A good research proposai describes situation of problem, problem area, justification, methodology adopted for data collection, analysis, expected results and institution/ organisation that may use the outcome.

7.2. HOW TO WRITE RESEARCH PROPOSAL / PROJECT

Some Starting Points for a Good Research Proposal

- Provides a realistic plan for investigation of your research question.
- Provides justification of a methodological perspective, and methods of investigation.
- Provides data which has the capacity to answer your research question.
- Adequately considers relevant ethical issues.

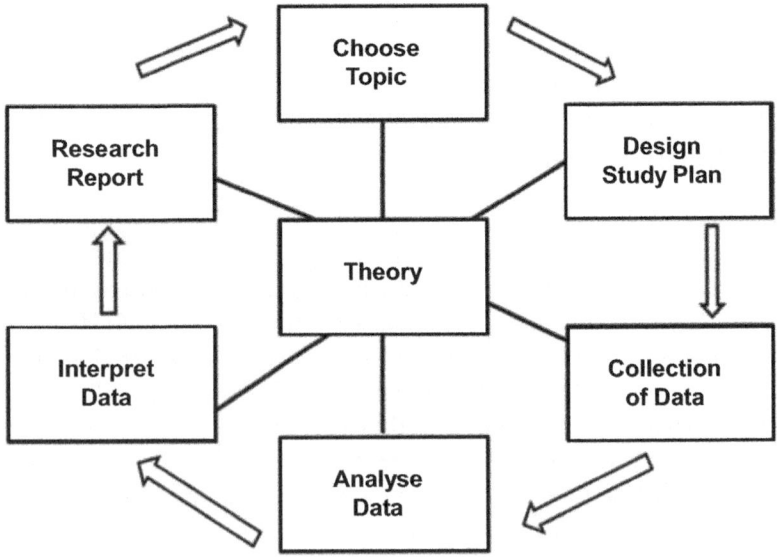

Methods or Methodology

- Methods are the techniques/ procedures used to collect and analyse data.

How to Write Research Proposal

- Methodology refers to discussions of how research is done, or should be done, and the critical analysis of methods of research.

Some Questions to be Pondered

- What's my research question?
- What theories, concepts, models inform my research?
- What kind of data will need to be answering my question?
- How will I collect this data?
- What ethical issues are relevant to my research?
- What are the strengths and limitations of my research?
- How much can I reasonably achieve in my research?
- How will my work be judged?

"a question well asked is a question half answered": the way the question (or hypothesis) is stated shows what data will be necessary to answer (or test) it and probably suggests also how and from where or from whom the data will be obtained.

Developing a Research Question

- Having come up with some prototype questions now refine
- Examine the scope of your questions
- Separate major and subsidiary questions
- Is each question necessary?
- Refine the wording of your questions

Refining your Questions

- Beware of the tendency toward bigger and more questions

Consider Carefully the Verbs you use in Your Question

- Explore (initial description)
- Describe (detailed account)
- Explain (establish the factors responsible)
- Understand (establish reasons)
- Predict (using an explanation to postulate future outcomes)

- Change (to actively intervene)
- Evaluate (assess if desired outcomes are achieved)

After Finalising the Research Question - Two Questions

- WHAT research strategy will be used?
- WHERE will the data come from?

A typical Research Proposal / Project have following skeletal structure; however, you have to use format provided by funding agency:

i. Topic or Research Problem or Research Question
ii. Summary of the Proposal
iii. Background and Justification
iv. Objectives
v. Hypothesis to be tested
vi. Review of Literature
vii. Methods
viii. Expected Output
ix. Time Budget
x. Financial Budget
xi. References
xii. Biography of the investigator(s)

Some Tips

A research proposal may be of following Types:

- Research proposal
- Grant proposal

Be Sure You are Ready to Write

- The idea must be good and must fit what the funding agency wants (see the pattern of projects awarded by funding agencies in their websites.)
- Proposal must be scientifically sound
- Outline a plan and review it carefully

How to Write Research Proposal

- Consider what personnel, money, equipment, time is needed and how it fits into the rest of your work load

Prepare for Questions and Answers Related to

i. Originality and scientific merit or benefit to the grantor
ii. Importance to the discipline or the immediate problem
iii. Feasibility
iv. Rationale and methodology
v. Ability and experience of the investigators
vi. Budget, facilities, and time required
vii. Appearance and adherence to guidelines

Justification is Based on

1. Reason and logic
2. Preliminary research
3. Scientific principles
4. Previous research (literature)
5. Feasibility of methods
6. Use of or benefit from the results

Additional Considerations

Your proposal may be rejected, so reduce your frustration by recognizing the beneficial side effects of the followings:

- Writing skills, knowledge on the subject, literature, resubmission

The Written Research Proposal

- Helps to plan the work in advance
- To review what is done
- To foresee the pitfalls ahead of you
- To remain on the right track (objectives – goals)
- Can serve as 'draft' for thesis or papers

7.3. A TYPICAL FORMAT FOR RESEARCH PROPOSAL

I. Cover page:[2]

Mekelle University
College of Natural and Computational Sciences
Department of Biology
Research Project Proposal

A Study on Fuel Wood Consumption Pattern and Feasability Analysis to Introduce Lowcost Energy-efficient Pressure Cooker: A Case Study of Households In Mekelle, Tigray, Ethiopia

Investigator

Ekwal Imam (PhD)

Department of Biology, CNCS, Mekelle University, Mekelle, Ethiopia.
Email<ekwalimam01@gmail.com

January, 2012

II. Research Project:[3]

A STUDY ON FUEL WOOD CONSUMPTION PATTERN AND FEASABILITY ANALYSIS TO INTRODUCE LOWCOST ENERGY-EFFICIENT PRESSURE COOKER: A CASE STUDY OF HOUSEHOLDS IN MEKELLE, TIGRAY, ETHIOPIA

III. Short Summary of the Project: [4]

The Federal Democratic Republic of Ethiopia has clearly put in its Energy policy document that it envisages for transforming the energy consumption pattern from the traditional to modern fuel and energy conservation in all types of uses. On the other hand, conservation of energy through copying suitable technologies is one of the target areas of the five years growth and transformation plans of Ethiopia. It is reported that consumption of electricity for all purpose is highly unaffordable for urban households in Ethiopia. Therefore, like other developing countries of Africa, Ethiopia experienced heavy dependence on a traditional energy source that is biomass mainly forest. In Ethiopia, consumption of biomass as source of household energy has shown an annual increment of 2.5% over the last two decades. This phenomenon coupled with energy in efficient fuel wood and charcoal consumption pattern has had serious degradation on the forest resource and resulted in overall ecological imbalance. According to some estimates, the proportion of land under forest cover has declined to less than 3%. Apart from this, energy inefficient traditional fuel wood consumption pattern has negative environmental, economic and health impacts.

The energy balance of the country as of 1995/96 reveals that total energy consumption in Ethiopia was estimated at about 50 million tones of wood equivalent. This calls for attention geared towards analyzing the existing pattern of fuel wood and charcoal consumption and look for possibilities of adopting low cost and energy efficient cookers. If such measures are not going to be instituted the existing poor energy consumption pattern will continue resulting in removal of the remaining fragmented patches of forests which may again result in household energy crisis in the country.

Furthermore, large volume of smoke emanating from poor fuel wood consumption pattern is reported to cause health problems like respiratory diseases manly to women in the household. Energy inefficient long hour cooking of food items in open pans results in loss of heat labile nutrients which may again contribute its part for diseases due to vitamin and nutrient deficiency particularly in young age children. For instance, vegetables cooked for 10 to 20 minutes can lose more than 50 percent of their vitamin C content.

On the other hand, pressure cooker, because of its short cooking time, may preserve the nutrient content of foods better than other options and also save fuel wood consumption upto 66 percent.

The study will be conducted in Mekelle. Study is designed in such a manner that it will reveal existing consumption patterns of fuel wood and will identify factors significantly contributing to the exiting poor fuel wood or charcoal energy consumption pattern. Importance of introduction of low priced energy efficient pressure cooker will be explained at household level and wherever needed demonstrations will also be made. After that, opinion survey will be conducted to know the people's perception regarding pressure cooker. This study will help policy makers to prescribe measures that will strengthen the conditions that encourage use of modern fuel efficient equipment/vessels which may ultimately conserve the energy and forest resource. Furthermore, this study will provide information on basic income of people, existing consumption pattern of fuel wood, energy demand at household level and peoples opinion on pressure cooker. This information will be helpful in formulation and implementation of energy related policy such as subsidies, taxes and energy conservation measures.

IV. Research Work to Date (if any)[5]

The following are relevant credentials (research experiences) of **DR. EKWAL IMAM,** the principal investigator of this research project.

Dr. Imam worked as a **Research Associate** on a WWF-India sponsored project- *Directory of National Parks and Sanctuaries in Madhya Pradesh and* surveyed more than 35 National Parks and Sanctuaries of Madhya Pradesh. India.

Dr. Imam also worked as **Wildlife Consultant** for Vrindaban conservation Project, WWF-India. Later on he joined as **Project Supervisor** in Vrindaban (Mathura- UP) monkeys rehabilitation project, sponsored by WWF-India and trapped more than 600 rhesus monkeys and translocated them.

Dr. Imam persuaded his Ph.D. in primate behaviour and ecology.

Research Project in Hand: (i). Running a University Grant Commission sponsored Research project as Co-Principal Investigator on Monkey menace in Aligarh, India

Details of Publications

Book: 02
1. Primates of India
2. Biostatistics

International Paper: 05

National paper: 09

International Papers

1. **Imam, E.** (2011). Use of geospatial technology in evaluating landscape cover type changes in Chandoli National Park, India. *Computational Ecology and Software.* 1(2):95-111.
2. **Imam, E.** (2011). Mapping of Landscape Cover Using Remote Sensing and GIS in Chandoli National Park, India. *Momona Ethiopian Journal of Science.* 3(2): 80-95.
3. **Imam, E.,** SPS Kushwaha, Aditya Singh (2009). Evaluation of suitable tiger habitat in Chandoli National Park, India, using multiple logisric regression. *Ecological Modelling (Pub by ELSEVIER, USA).* **Impact Factor = 2.176**

4. **Imam, E.** (2005) Population status and conservation of Indian Peafowl *Pavo cristatus* in Aligarh, northern India. In: Fuller, R.A. and Browne, J.S. (Eds.) Galliformes 2004. Proceeding on International galliformes Symposium. World Pheasant Association, Fordingbridge, U.K. International

5. **Imam, E.,** Yahya, H.S.A. and Malik, I. (2002) A successful mass translocation of commensal Rhesus monkeys *Macaca mulatta* in Vrindaban. *Oryx* (UK). Vol 36(1): 87-93. **Impact Factor= 1.381.**

6. **Imam, E and Ahmed, A.** Population distribution of rhesus monkey *Macaca mulatta* and its menace in Aligarh district of Uttar Pradesh, India. (COMMUNICATED).

National Paper

7. **Imam,E.** and Ahmad, S. N. (2010) Predicting the Impact of Global Warming on Biodiversity Exitinction. In: K.K. Misra and P. Mishra (eds),*Global Warming- An Overview*, Commitee on Personality and Human Development, Orai, India,pp.42-55

8. **Imam, E.** and Iqbal Malik (2006). Rhesus monkey (*Macaca mulatta*),Problems in India and their management. In Vertebrate pest in Agriculture-India scenario. Ed. Shakunthala Sridhara. Pub. Scientific Publisher, Jodhpur.

9. **Imam, E.** and Yahya, H.S.A. (2006) Relationship between male hierarchism and reproductive behaviour in rhesus monkey *macaca mulatta*. *Journal of Ecobiology.* Vol. 19(2). 185-198.

10. Hilaluddin, Kaul, R., Hussain, M. S., **Imam, E.,** Shah J. N., Abbasi, F. and Tahir,S. A. (2005) Status and distribution of breeding cattle egret and little egret in Amroha using density method. *Current Science.* Vol. 88(8). 1239-1243. **Impacr Factor= 0.8**

11. **Imam, E.** and Yahya, H.S.A. (2003) A Behavioural relationship between Mother and Infant in Rhesus Monkey *Macaca mulatta* of Aligarh District, Northern India. Abstract in *28th Conference of the Ethological Society of India*, Dept of Zoology, Sarah Tuker College, Tirunelveli, Tamil Nadu, India

12. **Imam, E.** & Yahya, H.S.A. (2002). Management of monkey problems in Aligarh Muslim University campus, Uttar Pradesh *Journal of Zoos' Pint.*Vol 17(1): 685-687

13. **Imam, E.**, Malik, I. and Yahya, H.S.A. (2001) Translocation of Rhesus monkey from Airforce Station, Gurgaon (Haryana) to Natural forest of Firozpur-Jhirkha) (Haryana), India. *Journal of Bombay Natural History Society.* Vol. 98(3): 355-359

14. **Imam, E.** and H.S.A. Yahya (1995) Population dynamics and distribution of rhesus monkey in Aligarh District. *Journal of Ecobiology.* 79(10): 1-9.

15. **Imam, E.** (1991). Translocation: A Proposal for the conservation and management of rhesus monkey in Aligarh district. *Zoos' Print.* Vol. VII (3): 3-4.

V. Proposed Research Project:

A) Background and Justification:[1]

Untill middle of the nineteenth century, wood was used everywhere as the principal source of energy. Particularly in less developed countries, wood has remain a dominant fuel and preferred form of domestic energy because it does not require complex expensive equipment. Fuelwood can be procured at no greater cost than the labour of collecting it. In addition most of its supply and use ocurrs outside the monetery economy, carried out largely by subsitence users (Arnold *et al.* 2003).

The impact of fuelwood collection on forest has been controversial, however its role in rural livelihood cannot be ignored. An early estimates indicated that there will be difference between fuelwood demand and supply. Therefore, a shortfall in fuelwood is assumed to result in serious negative socio-economic consequences for the rural poor people.

However, the dimenstion of the fuelwood situation that had the most direct implications for forestry was perception that it was a major factor leading to forest degradation and distruction. It is argued that, poor rural communities often had no alternative to wood fuel or other locally available organic fuel source.

Massive removal of woody biomass to meet fuelwood demand was believed to be a major factor underline environmnetal damage being experienced at various level (FAO). In many countries, public forest were historically managed to accommodate local fuel wood needs and forest department use to create village woodlots for human populations living distant from natural forests. This was one of the most important methods of reducing the anthropogenic pressure on natural forest areas as well as to fulfill the local demand of fuelwood. Howver, in developing counties like Ethiopia, establishment of village woodlots are either not in practice or very few programmes are implemented successfully. The reason may be that farmers are giving more priority to grow food crops than to community/village forestles.

Ethiopia with a population of over 70 million is one of the poorest countries in the world and depends heavily on traditional biomass fuels, including wood, crop residues, charcoal and dung, for 95% of its energy needs. The country's dependence on biomass fuel remains one of the highest in Africa (EFAP, 1993).

Woody biomass is the largest source of energy supply and if present trends continue there will be difference between fuelwood demand and supply. This may result in serious negative socio-economic consequences for the rural poor people.

Biomass use for household energy adversely affects crop production and productivity. With increased depletion of woody vegetation for fuel, heightened erosion of top soil has become glaringly evident; diminishing the production potential of cultivated land. At the same time, with increased use of crop residues and dung to compensate for the increasing scarcity and cost of firewood, natural fertilizers are being removed from the soil, leading to a progressive fall in crop yields.

The negative consequences of a heavy dependence on biomass fuel as a source of household energy are not restricted to the environment and crop production. Equally worrying is the fact that activities relating to the supply and use of biomass fuel have hazardous effects on human health, ranging from trauma to acute respiratory infection (Fekerte, 1991; WHO, 1992). During the preparation of cowdung cake as an alternative source of energy, women and children may have risk of being exposed to various zoonotic infections. The use of such inferior smokier fuel like cowdung cake and crop residues may also damage eyes and lungs of the rural communities. Not only this, the less fuel wood supply may also hamper the cooking of food which may directly affect supply of nutrition.

However, the dimenstion of the fuelwood situation that had the most direct implications for forestry was having perception that it was a major factor leading to forest degradation and distruction. It is argued that, as the poor rural communities often had no alternative to wood fuel or other locally available organic fuel source.

Massive removal of woody biomass to meet fuelwood demand was believed to be a major factor underline environmnetal damage being experienced at various level (FAO 1978).

No doubt fuelwood collection is causing degradation of the forest, but its role in energy supply as well as income generation for the poor can not be denied in Ethioia. During the preliminary pilot survey it was recorded by one of the authors that Mekelle city is becoming one of the centres for fuelwood market. Hundreds of donkeys loaded with fuelwood can be seen in the morning hours of periodical markey days coming from several directions of the city. This shows magnitudes of fuelwood consumption in Mekelle itself (Pers. comm).

A prelimanary survey conducted by one of the authors revealed that pressure cookers are potentially efficient for saving cooking time and fuel wood consumption upto 66 %. It is reported that cooking food for shorter periods of time results in less nutrient loss than longer cooked meals. Fruits and vegetables cooked for 10 to 20 minutes can lose more than 50 percent of their vitamin C content, According to World's Healthiest Foods, Microwave and pressure cooker cooking, because of its short cooking time, may preserve the nutrient content of foods better than other options (Anonymous 2012).

The proposed study is small efforts towards reducing the fuelwood consumption and hence conserving the energy.

B) Objectives of the Project: [2]

1. To estimate the total amount of fuelwood/charcoal extraction from the nearby area of mekelle city.
2. To identify plant species frequently extracted for fuelwood/charcoal.
3. To study the consumption pattern of fuelwood in Mekelle city
4. To analyze the feasability for the introduction of lowcost fuel-efficient pressure cooker at households level.

a) Hypothesis (Optional)

Increased consumption of traditional fuel may leads to more extraction of fuel-wood from forest and country side area.

b) Review of Literature (Optional): [3]

Almost 2 billion people are dependent on biomass fuel and all of these are in low income countries (Anderson, 1996). World Bank (1989) shows that the annual growth rates in modern energy consumption have been on the decrease in Sub-Saharan Africa; the annual growth rate decreased from 7 percent between 1965 and 1970, to 2.2 percent between 1980 and 1987. This has direct implication for greater reliance on the traditional sources of energy despite the countries' interest to insure energy transition. As a result, fuel wood gathering is one of the major contributory factors to deforestation, which is already claiming about 10 Million hectares of forest each year in the developing world (World Bank, 1984). Considering fuel wood consumption pattern and energy conservation measure, many works have been done in Ethiopia. In 1986, Dennis worked in African countries and suggested that tree stocks are declining. Whereas, World Bank recorded that in Adis Ababa (Ethiopia) price of fuel-wood had increased ten times from 9USD to 90 USD per tone during 1973-1983.

Considering the high level of fuelwood consumption, Federal Democratic Republic of Ethiopia has clearly put in its Energy policy document (1994) that it envisages for transforming the energy consumption pattern from the traditional to modern fuel and energy conservation in all types of uses. It has also stressed rational development and exploitation of indigenous energy sources such as hydroelectric powers, and natural gas. A study on household energy demand in urban Ethiopia was carried out by Asmerom (1991). EFAP (1993) estimated the proportion of land under forest cover and reported that forest cover had declined to less than 3%. In 1997, Mekonnen studied the rural household fuel consumption pattern in Ethiopia.

Mekonnen (2000) opined that despite these all, consumption of biomass fuel has been increasing at average of forest degradation; annual increment of 2.5% was recorded in fuelwood consumption over the last two decades, whereas, similar study was conducted by Bereket *et al.* in 2001. During the same year, Bereket Kebede *et.al.* (2001) worked on affordability of fuels and patterns of energy demand in urban Ethiopia and suggested that electricity consumption is highly unaffordable for urban households in Ethiopia, due to this people are using fuelwood. In 2004, UN-DESA conducted an assessment of energy consumption trends in the African continent and reported that the key challenge facing Africa is not to increase energy consumption per se, but to ensure access to cleaner energy services, preferably through energy efficiency and renewable energy thus promoting sustainable consumption (UN-DESA Report 2004).

Similarly, the present study is proposed for analyzing the feasibility to introduce low-cost energy efficient pressure cooker. This is an effort in the direction of energy conservation, which may reduce the pressure on biomass fuel and at large it will be helpful in conserving the forest resources at country level and environmental impact at global level.

Mekelle is a city in northern Ethiopia and the capital of the Tigray Region. It is located some 650 kilometers north of the capital, Addis Ababa, at latitude and longitude 13°29?N 39°28?E13.483°N 39.467°E Coordinates: 13°29?N 39°28?E13.483°N 39.467°E with an elevation of 2084 meters above sea level. Its total human population is 201528 (2008).

Study will be conducted using stratified sampling and households survey will be made in randomly selected kebelle. Total number of households to be surveyed will be determined during the execution of the project.

c) Methodology:[10][11]

The study is based on primary source of data. The data will be collected using questionnaire.

Estimation of Fuelwood Charcoal/Extraction

A survey of wood market situated near Kebele-17 of Mekelle city will be done during the periodical market days. For estimating the fuelwood/charcoal extaction, number of Donkeys carrying fuelwood/charcoal will be counted. The weight of wood-logs' bunch will also be considered. The total amount of fuelwood/charcoal extraction will also be estimated by interviewing the fuelwood/charcoal dealers. The diameter of wood/charcoal logs will be estimated to know the age of trees extracted for fuelwood/charcoal.

Consumption Pattern of Fuelwood

The city will be divided into different zones based on Kebele. From each zone about 10% of total households will be selected for data collection on consumption pattern of fuelwood/charcoal as well as on socio-economic benefits. We will select 10% of total restaurent/coffee houses/kefeteria present in the particular zone for collecting data on commercial use of fuelwood/charcoal.

Indentification of Plant Species Most Frequently Extracted

The person selling/trading the fuelwood/charcoal will be interviewed randomly to know about the local name of the plant and further cross checking will be done with the help of flora book of the region.

Survey to Analyze Feasibility for Introduction of Cooker

Structured interviews will be administered to the randomly selected household to gather data on the feasibility and scope of introduction of low cost energy-efficient pressure cooker. First respondents at households level will be made aware about pressure cooker in terms of cost of pressure cooker, time taken for cooking of a particular food item, percentage saving in fuel wood, nutrient conservation and health safety. After that people will be interviewed to know their opinion regarding the utility of pressure cooker which is capable of saving time, energy and taste of the food.

Data Analysis and Data Presentation

Data collected on prescribed questionnaire will be interred to computer using "Microsoft Office EXCEL". "Z" test will be used for normalization of data. Statistical tests like t-test, ANOVA, Chi-square, etc. will be used to study the relation and differences among various variables. For this SPSS software will be used.

After analysis the results will be presented in the form of graph, table and diagram to show the relation as well as variations among the variables.

d) Expected Output[12]

It is expected that from this study we may able to generate information on the pattern of fuel-wood consumption among all different sectors of the society. We will also be able to produce data on impact of fuel-wood collection/trade on socio-economic condition of the poor villagers as well as people involved in its trade.

The study will provide baseline data on anthropogenic (fuel wood/charcoal extraction) pressure responsible for forest degradation.

The data may be used by government agency/NGOs while making the policy related to energy consumption pattern in the country. The outcome will also be helpful in identifying the household while planning to provide alternate energy sources in the future. At least one article will be published on peer reviewed international journal out of this study and 2 PG (Zoology)/ UG students will be involved for their thesis work.

e) Time Schedule : [13]

S.N	Major Activities	Months/Year	Remark
1.	Procurement of consumables	January, 2012	Biology Deptt
2.	Pilot survey and delineation of study sites	February/ 2012	
3.	Collection of sampled data on pattern of fuel consumption at households level	March-May/ 2012	
4.	Survey of households to know their opinion regarding introduction of low-cost fuel-efficient pressure cooker.		
4.	Data analysis and write up of the manuscript for publication	June/ 2012	
4.	Reporting the research out put to the CNCS and sending the manuscript for publication	July-August/ 2012	

f) Duration:

The project will start in February 2012 and end in June, 2012 (a total of 6 months). Two additional months, July and August, 2012 will be utilized for reporting the research out put to the CNCS as well as preparing and sending the manuscript for publication.

VI. References:[15]

How to Write Research Proposal

VII. Collaborating Researchers & Institutions

This project will be executed in collaboration with group of researchers with different expertise from different institutions.

1. Kindeya Gebrehiwot (PhD), College of Dry Land agriculture and natural Resource, MU, Mekelle.
2. Tigray Burea of Agriculture (Forestry Division), Mekelle.
3. Tigray Burea of Energy and Mining, Mekelle.

VIII. Facilities and Funding

Computer Lab of Department of Biology (College NCS) will be utilized for data entry and analysis. The funding obtained from recurrent budget of the CNCS will be utilized for per dime/ travel allowance and purchasing of required materials & equipment, and stationary materials

IX Budget:[18]

Salaries /Per dime/ Travel allowances

No.	Description of expenses	No.	Unit Cost (ETB)	Total Cost (ETB)
1	Researchers' per dime	2	70 × 100 days	7,000.00
2	Per dime for field assistant	2	70 × 100 days	7,000.00
3	Per dime for medical laboratory technician	1	70 × 60 days	4,200.00
4	Salary for computer lab assistant	1	700/month/ 3 months	2,100.00
5	Car rent/ public transport / fuel cost			25,000.00

Sub Total = 45, 100.00

Purchases

No.	Description of expenses	No.	Unit Cost (ETB)	Total Cost (ETB)
1	Low Cost Pressure Cooker	5	500	2,500.00
2	Food items for cooking cooking demonstration (meat)	50kg	100/Kg	5,000.00
3	Stationery materials			1,000.00
				Sub Total = 8500.00

Summary of the Project Cost

No	Description of Expenses	Total expense (Birr)
1	Salaries/Per diem / Travel and Allowance	45,100.00
2	Purchases	8,500.00
3	Miscellaneous cost (10%)	5360.00
		Total cost = 58,960

X. Assurance of Principal Investigator

The undersigned agrees to accept responsibility for the scientific, ethical and technical conduct of the research project and for the provision of required progress reports as per terms and conditions of the University in effect at the time of grant, if grant is awarded as the result of this application

7.4. SUMMARY

Define the research problem

Different contents required for developing a research proposal

Typical example of a research proposal

Chapter – 8

Scientific Communication

Studying this chapter will enable us:
- *To know the concept of Thesis writing*
- *To know what are the basic pre-requisite to write a good Thesis*
- *To know the format of a typical Thesis*

8.1. INTRODUCTION

The existence of Science could be in danger, if scientists did not record experiment performed, data collected and resuit obtained. Scientific writing doesn't mean to only keep records of progress and information, but to actually publish the results of studies in scientific journals. While keeping records is quite easy to do, publishing scientific papers can be really difficult, and especially for young researchers who are just starting to discover the world of scientific publications. A scientific writing is a method of communication, an attempt to tell others about some specific data that you have gathered and what you think those data mean in the context of your research. The rules of writing a scientific paper are rigid and are différent Uorr\ those that apply when we write an English theme. Scientific paper must be written clearly and concisely so that readers with backgrounds similar to yours can understand easily what you have done and how you have done it. The ultimate aim of most scientists is to publish their research findings in professional scientific reports. This includes peer-reviewed journal articles, which report original findings and contribute to the global pool of scientific knowledge. Scientists spend their time writing proposals, planning research, undertaking experiments, analysing data, tracing research, and reading related articles. Published reports and journal articles provide evidence of this dedication. Therefore, a scientific report is not simply some extra work that is done at the end of a project; it is an important historical document that provides evidence of work to the wider scientific community.

8.2. HOW TO PREPARE A THESIS

A thesis in the sciences is supposed to present the candidate's original research. Its purpose is to prove that the candidate is capable of doing and communicating original research. Therefore, a proper thesis should be like a scientific paper, which has the same purpose. A thesis should exhibit the same form of disciplined writing that would be required in a journal publication. Unlike the scientific paper, the thesis may describe more than one topic, and it may present more than one approach to some topics. The thesis may present all or most of the data obtained in the student's thesis-related research. Therefore, the thesis usually can be longer and more involved than a scientific paper. But the concept that a thesis must be a bulky 200-page to me is dead wrong. Most 200-page thesis contains maybe 100 pages of good science. The other 100 pages comprise turgid descriptions of insignificant details.

There are few rules for writing a thesis. If you do not have rules to follow, go to your departmental library and examine the thesis submitted by previous post graduates of the department, especially those who have gone on to fame and fortune. Generally, a thesis should be written in the style of a review paper. Its purpose is to review the work that led to your degree. Your original data (whether previously published or not) should of course be incorporated, by all necessary experimental detail. Each of several sections might actually be designed along the lines of a research paper (Introduction, Materials and Methods, Results, Discussion). Overall, however, the parts should fit together like those of a monographic review paper.

Start with and work from a carefully prepared outline. In your outline and in your thesis, you will of course describe in detail your own research results. It is also customary to review all related work. Further, there is no bar in a thesis, as there may be in state-of-the-art review papers, to old tradition, so it is often desirable to go back into the history of your subject. You might thus compile a really valuable review of the literature of your field.

Give special attention to the Introduction in the thesis. You have to clarify what problem you attacked, how and why you selected that problem, how you attacked it, and what you learned during the course of your studies. It would be wise to begin writing thesis long before it is due. In fact, when a particular set of experiments or some major facet of the work has been completed, one should write it up while it is still fresh in the mind. If saved everything until the end, one may find that you have forgotten important details. Worse, you may find that you just don't have time to do a proper writing job. If you have not done much writing previously, you will be amazed at what a painful and time-consuming process it is. You are likely to need a total of 3 months to write the thesis, on a relatively full-time basis. You will not have full time, however, nor can you count on the ready availability of your thesis advisor. Allow 6 months at a minimum.

The research process

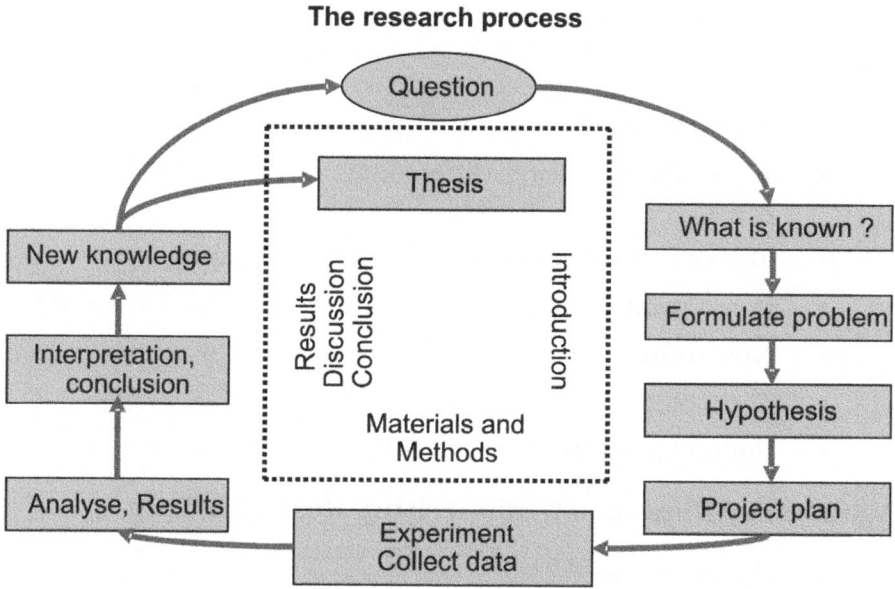

Remember, your thesis will bear your name. A tightly written, coherent thesis will help you in good start of your career. The writers of good thesis try to avoid difficult vocabulary and always use simple language. Be particularly careful in writing the Abstract of your thesis. The Abstracts of thesis from most institutions are published in *Dissertation Abstracts*, thus being made available to the larger scientific community.

- Identification of a question/problem
- What is known-what is not known???

- Identify a hypothesis
- Set up a research plan
- Collect information
- Manage data, discuss
- Write and review your thesis

Make an Outline

- Structured order of headings and subheadings – with keywords – chart
- A working outline – a tool to help
- Discuss your outline with others (co-author, supervisor, colleague ...)

A Good Title

- It should be Informative: describe the subject
- It should be specific: differentiate your research from other research
- It should be concise: say only what is necessary
- If you want to have 'Two-part' title, it should be like this :
- New technologies for constructions: A novel approach
- Technologies for constructions: A review
- But do notuse numbers (I, II, III .... 1, 2, 3 ...)

Avoid these Pharages While Writing Research Title

- Observations of ...
- Studies of ...
- Investigations ...
- Examinations of ...
- A note on ....
- Effects of ...
- Influence of ...
- Estimation of ...

- Prediction of ...
- Impact of ...
- Modelling of ...
- Evidence of ...
- Control of ...
- Measurement of ...
- Use of ...

Copyright

"The author and supervisor give permission to put this thesis to disposal for consultation and to copy parts of it for personal use. Any other use falls under the limitations of copyright, in particular the obligation to explicitly mention the source when citing parts out of this thesis"

Date + names + signatures

General Acknowledgements

- You can aknowledge your institution, organization, research project, source of funds

Specific Acknowledgements can be Used for

- Promotor, colleague students or technicians
- Parents, friends ....

Dedication

You can dedicate your work to any one

Remember Following Points

- Use decimal system for chapters (e.g. 1.1. not 1.a.)
- No underlining
- Avoid subdivisions up to the 5th degree
- Keep the length within a few pages

Abstract

Descriptive abstract

- Describes the content, needs to be accompanied by the document
- Is helpful for the reader to decide to read the entire thesis
- Start with motivation or justification
- State the objective, aim, or purpose
- Summarise the essential methods
- Summarise important results
- End with important conclusions and impact
- Make the abstract stand alone
- Be specific and concise: 200 to 250 words

Criteria for Effective Writing

Criterion

- Clear
- Complete
- Correct
- Efficient

Meaning

Reader gets the message
Questions are answered
Message is accurate
Saves reader time

Verb Tenses for Abstract

- Motivation and justification: **present**
    - Lack of water is the most important ...
- Literature: **past/present perfect**
    - Studies showed that ....
    - Studies have shown that...–

- Objectives: **past**
  - The objective was to model ...
- Material and methods: past
  - Soil was sampled from ....
- Results and discussion: **past/present**
  - Uptake of nitrogen was ..., which means that
  - Figure 5 shows ...
  - In Fig. 7 data are ....
- Conclusions: **present**
  - Calculations suggest that

Be Coherent

Coherence refers to the logical sequence of sentences within a paragraph
- Discuss only one subject in a paragraph
- Put the topic sentence first
- Tell the reader what to expect
- Be consistent in your style
- Use the same organisational pattern for successive sentences

How to Start Writing

Introduction

- Motivate and justify the research
- Give a state of the art
  - Summarize relevant literature
- State what has NOT been done
  - Where is the gap in the literature?
- State the objectives or hypothesis
  - What's the point of this research ?
- Finally, what will be the content of the thesis

Literature Review

- Characteristics of a review: work from several sources is reported, rather than from one experiment or research programme
- Common in journals and conference proceedings, in university training
- Use literature review in shorter form in Introduction of a paper
- Use literature review in longer form in thesis
- Identify key-words & phrases of your work
- Search: - in the library (databases)
- - websites
- - local papers and books
- Record all found information
- Organize your information according to topics
- Compare information
- Be critical
- Identify contrasting information and try to find an explanation
- Identify gaps in the knowledge

Materials and Methods

- Give a clear, complete description of all methods used (biological, chemical, analytical, statistical.)
  - Organize the methods logically, by tasks
  - Use specific and informative language
- Include enough information, but not more than necessary, so that the research can be repeated

Results

- Summarise and illustrate the findings logically with tables and figures
- Figures & Tables: see further
- Do not repeat data from the tables or figures in the text

- Mean yield for cultivar A is X and mean weight for cultivar B is Y
- Do integrate data with the text
  - Mean yield of cultivar A was higher than mean yield of cultivar B
- Do not interpret the data or draw conclusions in the 'results' section

An Effective Results Section

i. Not all results need to be given – give relevant only
ii. Order results chronologically or by importance
iii. Text should complement tables and figures, do not repeat
iv. Give clear description of the magnitude of response or difference
v. Data should be accurate and consistent throughout the text
vi. Summarize statistical analysis and report the actual P values for all primary analysis
vii. Use the past tense to refer to results
viii. Number the figures and tables according to their appearance
ix. Provide a clear title; each table and figure could stand separately form the text
x. Write with accuracy, brevity and clarity

Tables

- Upper –lower case type is easier to read than all upper case letters
- Round data to simplify; use common units
- Avoid vertical lines between columns
- Avoid horizontal lines, except when needed
- Space after every five lines
- Use a logical format: portrait or landscape
- Emphasize similarities and differences
- Goup similar items

- Separate dissimilar items
- Arrange comparisons vertically
- Make the content concise
- Avoid repetitive information
- Avoid redundant information
- Self-contained
- Use foot notes freely
- Title above the table; no full stop at the end of the title

8.3. HOW TO WRITE SCIENTIFIC RESEARCH PAPER

What is a Research Paper?

There are two kinds of research papers:
  I. Primary or experimental research paper
  II. Secondary or review research paper

Writing a Scientific Research Paper

Primary or experimental research papers describe an experiment performed by the author. The investigation may employ a rigorously controlled lab experiment, a field experiment, a theoretical/mathematical investigation, or simply some new scientific observations. The key is that the body of the paper is about a novel investigation conducted by the author.

Organizing the Paper

The first step is to find a general topic. Find a relatively narrow topic that interests you. When you find a topic, go to preliminary survey of literature. Pick prominent journals in the appropriate field of biology. Consult your instructor for a list of respected journals in that field. Read the abstracts of those papers with interesting titles. If you find a good article, this may help narrow your topic and serve as a good research resource. Journals provide good review articles in many fields of science. For example, in *Science* these are called "Perspectives" or "Reviews". In *Nature* these are called "News and Views". The topic headings should refer to the actual concepts or ideas covered in that section.

Breadth of the topic	Choose a topic with enough background materials available to make your project factual and interesting, but not so broad that you cannot address the topic thoroughly. It is best to think of the topic as a thesis, hypothesis, or question to be proven, tested, or answered.
Examples of bad topics	"Cancer" is too broad of a topic. "Is Tibetan Chanting a Cure for Cancer?" probably has not been well investigated scientifically.
Examples of good topics	"The use of Taxol from the Pacific Yew to Treat Ovarian Cancer" is a fairly concise topic thesis that should yield enough scientific data for a decent project. "Taxol from the Pacific Yew is Effective in Treating Ovarian Cancer" is a concise topic hypothesis. "Is Taxol from the Pacific Yew Effective in Treating Ovarian Cancer?" is a concise topic question.

Preliminary Survey of Literature

What to search	General Internet searches using search engines such as "www.Google.com" may yield much information on your topic. However, you will need to base your work on more reliable and scientifically legitimate sources of information obtained from primary literature and other appropriate technical references.
	Also, feel free to consult with your instructor or someone else who is knowledgeable in the topic area that interests you.
	Use the electronic card catalog in Library. You can even access card catalogs from other campuses. You may want to do your searches using key words
	Under "Subject Resources", select "Biology". There are several excellent online literature databases to search. Abstracts of articles are a good source of preliminary information about journal articles
What to look	Current research questions
	Recent breakthroughs of public interest
	Once you've identified a subject for your project you need to formulate a topic question, hypothesis or thesis.
Finding relevant papers	You should relie on scientifically legitimate sources of information obtained from primary literature and other appropriate technical references.
	Do a more thorough job of searching using various online resources
	Look up references in the Literature Cited section of a relevant article.
	Search for other articles by authors of key references.

	Science Citation Index (only opens from campus computers) is a very helpful way to locate more recent articles that cite a given paper. You can request for interlibrary loan also. However, you should allow at least two weeks for your requests to be filled.
Analyze the data you have collected	Which studies support your hypothesis/thesis/question? Do some studies support alternative hypotheses? Is there controversy in the scientific community over this topic, or general agreement? Collect relevant graphs, figures or tables that can be used in your presentation.

What Goes into Each Section

Section of the paper	What it should contain
Introduction & Background	• Make it brief (~1/5th of the paper's total length). • Grab the reader's interest while introducing the topic. • Explain the "big picture" relevance. • Provide the necessary background information.
Body of the Paper	• Experimental Evidence: Describe important results from recent primary literature articles. • Explain how those results shape our current understanding of the topic. • Mention the types of experiments done and their corresponding data, but do not repeat the experimental procedure step for step. • Point out and address any controversies in the field. • Use figures and/or tables to present your own synthesis of the original data or to show key data taken directly from the original papers.
Conclusion	• Summarize your major points. • Point out the significance of these results. • Discuss the questions that remain in the area. • Keep it in brief.
Literature Cited	• Cite the references used in manuscript according to the journal's guidelines.

Overview of the Paper

A research paper should consist of four general sections

- Introduction

- The body of the paper
- Conclusion and future directions
- Literature cited

It is considered that a research paper should be arranged in the manner of IMRAD that is;

I: Introduction
M: Material and Methods
R: Results
D: Discussion

How to Cite References used in Text

There are two rules to follow in the References section:

Reference for published data

One should list only significant, published references. A paper that has been accepted for publication can be listed in Literature Cited, citing the name of the journal followed by "In press."

Reference for unpublished data

References to unpublished data, abstracts, thesis, and other secondary materials should not clutter up the References. If such a reference seems absolutely essential, one may add it parenthetically or as a footnote in the text. Check all parts of every reference against the original publication before the manuscript is submitted and perhaps again at the proof stage. There are far more mistakes in the References section of a paper than anywhere else. And don't forget, as a final check, make sure that all references cited in the text are indeed listed in the Literature Cited and that all references listed under Literature Cited are indeed cited somewhere in the text.

Reference Styles

Journals vary considerably in their style of handling references. Some journals print titles of articles and some do not. Some insist on inclusive pagination, whereas others print first pages only. The smart author writes out references on 3" by 5" cards, usually in full or insert (feed) the full information into a computer file. Then, in preparing a manuscript, he or she has all the needed information. Even if you know that the journal to which you plan to submit your manuscript uses a short form (no article titles, for example), you would still be wise to establish your reference list in the complete form. This is good practice because (1) the journal you selected may reject your manuscript, resulting in your decision to submit the manuscript to another journal, perhaps one with more demanding requirements, and (2) it is more than likely that you will use some of the same references again in later research papers, review articles (and most review journals demand *full* references), or books. When you submit a manuscript for publication, make sure that the references are presented according to the Instructions to Authors. If the references are radically different, the editor and referees may assume that this is a sign of previous rejection or, at best, obvious evidence of lack of care.

Although there are an almost infinite variety of reference styles, most journals cite references in one of three general ways that may be referred to as

- A. Name and year,
- B. Alphabet-number and
- C. Citation order

A. Name and Year System

The name and year system (often referred to as the Harvard system) has been very popular for many years and is used in many journals and books. Its big advantage is convenience to the author, because the references are unnumbered, references can be added or deleted easily. No matter how many times the reference list is modified, eg., "Smith and Jones (1998)" remains exactly that. If there are two or more "Smith and Jones (1998)" references, the problem is easily handled by listing the first as "Smith and Jones (19980a)," the second as "Smith and Jones (I 998b)," etc. The disadvantage to the reader occurs when (often in the Introduction) a large number of references has to be cited within one sentence or paragraph. Sometimes the reader must jump over several lines of parenthetical references before he or she can again pick up the text. Even two or three references, cited together, can be distracting to the reader. The disadvantage to the publisher is obvious, that is increased cost. When "Smith, Jones, and Higginbotham (1998)" is converted to "(7)," composition (typesetting) and printing costs can be reduced.

Because some papers are written by large number of authors, most journals that use name and year have a "*et al.*" rule. Names are always used in citing papers with either one or two authors, e.g., "Smith (1998)," "Smith and Jones (1998)." If the paper has three authors, list all three the first time the paper is cited, e.g., "Smith, Jones, and McGillicuddy (1998)." If the same paper is cited again, it can be shortened to "Smith *et al.* (1998)." When a cited paper has four or more authors, it should be cited as "Smith *et al.* (1998)" even in the first citation. In the References section, some journals prefer that all authors be listed (no matter how many); other journals cite only the first three authors and follow with "*et al.*"

B. Alphabet-Number System

This system of citation by number from an alphabetized list of references, is a modification of the name and year system. Citation by numbers keeps printing expenses within bounds; the alphabetized list, particularly if it is a long list, is relatively easy for authors to prepare and readers (especially librarians) to use. Some authors who have habitually used name and year tend to dislike the alphabet-number system, claiming that citation of numbers cheats the reader. Title reader should be told, so the argument goes, the name of the person associated with the 'cited phenomenon; sometimes, the reader should also be told the date, on the grounds that an 1897 reference might be viewed differently than a 1997 reference.

Fortunately, these arguments can be overcome. As you cite references in the text, decide whether names or dates are important. If they are not, use only the reference number: "Pretyrosine is quantitatively converted to phenylalanine under these conditions (13)." If you want to feature the name of the author, do it within the context of the sentence: "The role of the carotid sinus in the regulation of respiration was discovered by Heymans (13)." If you want to feature the date, you can also do that within the sentence: "Streptomycin was first used in the treatment of tuberculosis in 1945 (13)."

C. Citation Order System

The citation order system is simply a system of citing the references (by number) in the order that they appear in the paper. This system avoids the substantial printing expense of the name and year system, and readers often like it because they can quickly refer to the references if they so desire in one-two-three order as they come to them in the text. It is a useful system for a journal that is basically a "note" journal, each paper containing only a few references. For long papers, with many references, citation order is probably not a good system. It is not good for the author, because of the substantial renumbering task that results from addition or deletion of references. It is not ideal for the reader, because the non-alphabetical presentation of the reference list may result in separation of various references to works by the same author.

Title and Inclusive Pages in References

Should article titles be given in references? Normally, you will have to follow the style of the journal. If the journal allows a choice, it is recommended to give complete references. By denoting the overall subjects, the article titles make it easy for interested readers (and librarians) to decide whether they need to consult none, some, or all of the cited references.

The use of inclusive pagination (first and last page numbers) makes it easy for potential users to distinguish between 1-page notes and 50-page review articles. Obviously, the cost, to you or your library, of obtaining the references, particularly if acquired as photocopies, can vary considerably depending on the number of pages involved.

Journal Abbreviations

Although journal styles vary widely, one aspect of reference citation has been standardized in recent years, i.e., journal abbreviations. As the result of widespread adoption of a standard (American National Standards Institute, 1969), almost all of the major primary journals and secondary services now use the same system of abbreviation. Previously, most journals abbreviated journal names, but there was no uniformity. The *Journal of the American Chemical Society* was variously abbreviated to "J. Amer. Chem. Soc.," "Jour. Am. Chem. Soc.," "J.A.C.S.: etc.

These differing systems posed problems for authors and publishers alike. Now there is essentially only one system, and it is uniform. The word "Journal" is now always abbreviated "J." (Some journals omit the periods (full stops) after the abbreviations). By noting a few of the rules, authors can abbreviate many journal titles, even unfamiliar ones, without reference to a source list. It is helpful to know, for example, that all "ology" words are abbreviated at the end letter of "l." ("Bacteriology" is abbreviated "Bacteriol. "; "Physiology" is abbreviated "Physiol.," etc). Thus, if one memorizes the abbreviations of words commonly used in titles, most journal titles can be abbreviated with ease. An exception to be remembered is that one-word titles *(Science, Biochemistry)* are never abbreviated.

Selected Journal Title Word Abbreviations

Word	Abbreviation	Word	Abbreviation
Abstracts	Abstr.	Bacteriology	Bacteriol.
Academy	Acad.	Bakterioiogie	Bakteriol.
Acta	No abbrev.	Berichte	Ber.
Advances	Adv.	Biochemical	Biochem.
Agriculture	Agric.	Biochimica	Biochim.

Citation in the Text

It is depressing that many authors use careless methods in citing the literature. A common offender is the "hand waving reference, in which author's work is referred as "Smith's elegant contribution" without any hint of what Smith reported or how Smith's results relate to the present author's results. If a reference is worth citing, the reader should be told why.

Even worse is the nasty habit some authors have of insulting the authors of previous studies. It is probably all right to say "Smith (1997) did not study .... " But it is not all right to say "Smith (1997) totally overlooked..

" or "Smith (1997) ignored ...

Some authors get into the habit of putting all citations at the end of sentences. This is wrong. The reference should be placed at that point in the sentence to which it applies.

Examples of Different Reference Styles

Name and Year System

- Day, R. A. 1998. How to write and publish a scientific paper. 5th ed. Phoenix: Oryx Press.
- Huth, E. J. 1986. Guidelines on authorship of medical papers. *Ann. Intern. Med.* 104: 269-274.
- Sproul, J., H. Klaaren, and F..Mannarino. 1993. Surgical teatment of Freiberg's infraction in athletes. *Am. J. Sports Med.* 21: 381-384.

Alphabet-Number System

1. Day, R. A. 1998. How to write and publish a scientific paper. 5th ed. Phoenix: Oryx Press.

2. Huth, E. J. 1986. Guidelines on authorship ofmedical papers. *Ann. Intern. Med.* 104:269-274.

3. Sproul, J., H. Klaaren, and F. Mannarino. 1993. Surgical treatment of Freiberg's infraction in athletes. *Am. J. Sports Med.* 21:381-384.

Citation Order System

1. Huth EJ. Guidelines on authorship of medical papers. *Ann Intern Med.* 1986; 104:269-74.

2. Sproul J, Klaaren H, Mannarino F. Surgical treatment of Freiberg's infraction in athletes. *Am J Sports Med* 1993; 21:381-4.

3. Day RA. How to write and publish a scientific paper. 5th ed. Phoenix: Oryx Press, 1998.

Other Ways of Writing References

- Kimura Y, Kido T, Takaku T, Sumoyoshi M, Baba K. (2004). Isolation of an anti-angiogenic substance from *Agaricus blazei* Murrill: its antitumor and antimetastatic actions. *Cancer Sci.* 95: 758-764.

- Fabricius, K and Alderslade, P, *Safi corals and seafans -A comprehensive guide to the tropical shallow water - genera of the central - west Pacific, the Indian ocean and the Red sea* - AIMS, New Litho, Surrey hills, Melbourne, Australia, (2001).

- Hornell.J, The study of Indian Molluscs - Part I - *J. Bom. Nat. Hist. Soc.,* (1976) Vol.48, pp 303-774.

8.4. HOW TO WRITE A REVIEW PAPER

Review research papers summarize the research that has been done in a particular area. Reviews generally do not introduce much new information or new results, but rather synthesize a larger body of work, providing a new perspective on a field or question.

A review paper is not a 'book report' or an annotated list of experiments in a particular field, but demands a considerable, complete literature review. However, beyond just reporting the results and conclusions of other studies is not sufficient; the review must integrate, interpret and expand these conclusions. Often, articles must be read over and over again to really understand the subtle relevance of a particular result or conclusion. Then, the independent conclusions of separate investigations must be combined into a cohesive presentation. They must be contrasted and compared if there are conflicting conclusions. Apparent conflicts should be resolved through a new outlook or interpretation. Review papers often take historical perspectives, describing how a field changed as more information was accumulated. Or, review papers may focus on 'the state of the art' in a particular field; interpreting divergent results and suggesting an appropriate avenue for future research.

Who writes review articles? Usually, it is the experts in a particular field. They have the experience and knowledge to critically evaluate experiments and organize them in a new provocative way; perhaps incorporating them into a new, unifying theory. Good review papers are not easy to write; if they were, more scientists would write them.

The purpose of a review paper is to concisely review recent progress in a particular topic. It creates an understanding of the topic for the reader by discussing the findings presented in recent research papers.

A review paper is not a "term paper" or book report. It is not merely a report on some references you found. Instead, a review paper synthesizes the results from several primary literature to produce a consistent argument about a topic or focused description of a field.

Follow the Instructions before Starting to Write Review Paper

Step 1: Search the library's online databases to find scholarly or peer-reviewed articles. You can also look in indexes available at the library.

Step 2: Read the entire article. Many journal articles can be quite complex and use complicated wording and statistics. You may need to read the article a few times before you get a full grasp of it.

Step 3 : Write a citation for the journal article at the top of the review. You can take help from American Psychological Association's (APA) style and consult its manual or the link under Resources for citation information. You will need the title of the article, the journal where the article is published, the volume and issue number, publication date, author's name and page numbers for the article.

Step 4: Write a summary of the article. This should be one to three paragraphs, depending on the length of the article. Include the purpose for the article, how research was conducted, the results and other relevant information from the article.

Step 5: Discuss the meaning or implication of the results of the study that the article is about. This should be one to two paragraphs.

This is where you offer your opinion on the article. Discuss any flaws with the article, how you think it could have been better and what you think it all means.

Step 6: Write one paragraph discussing how the author could expand on the results, what the information means in the big picture, what future research should focus on or how future research could move the topic forward. Discuss how knowledge in the area could be expanded.

Step 7: Cite any direct quotes or paraphrases from the article. Use the author's name, the year of publication and the page number (for quotes) in the in-text citation. Refer to the link in the Resources section to do this correctly.

A review is a comprehensive synthesis of results from a wide and complex set of studies; it is a synthesis of *findings* rather than ideas. Goal of a review paper is to help readers make sense of all available information.

Research reviews focus on primary sources: Original scientific experimentation reported in scientific journals. The quality of the review depends largely on the comprehensiveness of the literature search.

Examples of Scientific Reviews can be found in

- Scientific American
- Science in the "Perspectives" and "Reviews" sections
- Nature in the "News and Views" section
- Compilations of reviews such as:

    Current Opinion in Cell Biology

    Current Opinion in Genetics & Development

    Annual Review of Plant Physiology and Plant Molecular Biology

    Annual Review of Physiology

    Trends in Ecology & Evolution
- Almost every scientific journal has special review articles.

Scientists commonly use reviews to communicate with each other and the general public. There are a wide variety of review styles from ones aimed at a general audience (e.g., *Scientific American*) to those directed at biologists within a particular sub discipline (e.g., *Annual Review of Physiology*).

A key aspect of a review paper is that it provides the evidence for a particular point of view in a field. Thus, a large focus of your paper should be a description of the data that support or refute that point of view. In addition, you should inform the reader of the experimental techniques that were used to generate the data.

The emphasis of a review paper is interpreting the primary literature on the subject. You need to read several original research articles on the same topic and make your own conclusions about the meanings of those papers.

Generally a Review Paper has the following sections

- Title
- Abstract
- Introduction
- Body
- Conclusion
- Acknowledgements
- Literature Cited

Although you are not conducting an experiment in the physical sense, you should consider your paper a 'thought' experiment. You are going to read a body of information and provide a new outlook on a topic. You will not reveal a new scientific 'fact' as an experimenter would, but you will reveal a new idea or interpretation. Therefore, build your paper in a way an experimenter (researcher) use to do:

1) Research a topic and find a particular set of issues, results or opinions that seem in conflict.

2) Research this area in more detail and then think independently. Build an argument or thesis that either supports one side of the conflict or resolves it. This is the 'experimental' part of the work, and it is as unique as a new experiment.

Steps to Write a Review Paper

Ask a Question

For a topic on that you want to write a review paper, you must have to prepare a question. Usually it is a broad, unrefined question, because you haven't researched to finalize the topic.

Take notes in your own words. Keep the notes in a file (hard copy or soft copy). Record the complete citation, so you don't have to look it up again. Relate their findings to your question.

- Is your question relevant, or is it trivial?
- Is your question redundant (has it already been answered)?
- Who are the experts in the field? (You can use them later for author searches).
- What methods have been used to address these questions?
- Finally, what did they find?

Literature Review

Before you attempt an on-line search, go to the library and find general references on your topic. Introductory textbooks can be a big help to you at this stage, providing important background information is available in simple language. After you familiarize yourself with the background materials, proceed to the technical literature; this includes both primary research articles and secondary research articles by scientists working / worked on your topic. Your best bet here would be a review article. Again, before the computer search, go to the stacks and look for review series in your discipline. In ecology, for example, there is *Annuals Reviews of Ecology and Systematics*, *Advances in Ecological Research*, and *Trends in Ecology and Evolution*. Review articles are "gold mines" of relevant literature. By finding one good review article, you can save yourself hours at the computer terminal navigating through a complete on-line search. BE SMART Even if you have to pull volumes down one by one and check the table of contents, you will probably find a review article that is relevant to your topic. A good review article will: 1) integrate lots of articles. 2) show you what major research directions in the field, and 3) summarize the major conclusions. It would take you hours at the computer to filter through searches to locate all these articles

Abstract

Abstract is considered as a concise summary of the paper. Ideally, it should be short (roughly 3% of the length of the paper), and should include a sentence describing each of these topics:

- Objectives and Introduction (background)
- Methods

- Results
- Conclusions and discussion (relevance)

Again, the space limitations may force you to be selective. In addition, the methods and result may be difficult to describe completely in single sentences, and may require a larger fraction of the space budget. However, you must also include a conclusion sentence; what do the results from your research mean? If published, the abstract may appear in citation sources such as Biological Abstracts and Science Citation Index. It is the first thing someone will read, and it must be descriptive and interesting. The abstract demands clear, direct writing. When readers finish the abstract, they should be so intrigued by the experiment that they decide to read the entire paper. What search strategy do you use when you pick up a journal? You read down the titles. Then, you read the abstract. Here is where you try to gain the attention of the reader. If you do not succeed, your reader may not want to continue reading your paper. Abstracts are very difficult to write; it will take more time to write than any other paragraph in the whole paper.

Body of Paper

First develop the outlines. Outlines will be a big help to you at this stage. Don't be afraid to write your ideas done before they are perfectly formed. If you can get them down on paper, you can place them in a logical sequence and develop them into a flowing presentation. After your body is complete, you can move on to your introduction and conclusion.

Introduction

Your introduction should be short; perhaps a page in length. It is not labeled with a separate heading, it just focuses the reader on the issues you will describe or contrast in the body of your paper. It is not a review of the field; it merely establishes a common point of departure for readers with different levels of expertise. It should provide some justification for the paper (why the issue is important), and it should present the objective of the paper. Again, as in the experimental paper, an easy way to create a logical introduction is to direct the reader from broader background information to the specific issues that you will address.

Conclusion

Conclusion is particularly kept separately. In the conclusion, you should redefine the objective of the study and show how you satisfied these goals. It should strengthen the relationship between the ideas you have built in the body of the paper.

Acknowledgments

Thank the people who helped you in research designing or conducting the experiment, and review drafts. Also acknowledge any funding support, and the source.

Literature Cited/ References

This section contains bibliographical information on the references that were cited in the body of the paper. It is not a bibliography. List only those references that were actually cited in the body of the text. First, you must understand how to cite references in the body of the text.

When you are all done, set it aside for at least one day. Re-read your paper, sentence by sentence, as if you were reading it for the first time. Be hard on yourself; any improvements that you make at this stage will directly enhance the quality of your paper.

Formatting

Use double spacing, 12 pt. New Times Roman, and one inch margins. Page numbering in upper right is preferred.

Formatting the Review Paper

General Information

- 15-20 pages of text (not including figures and tables)
- Typed, double-spaced
- 12 point Times, Times New Roman, Palatino phont
- Margins 1.5" left, 1" top, 1" right, 1" bottom
- Indent each new paragraph 0.25"
- Must be in a bound folder with a transparent cover

Title Page

- Center title about 1/3 down the page in18-point font. Capitalize the first letter of each word except for articles (a, an, the), conjunctions (and, but, for) and prepositions (in, on, to)

Title of a Review Paper: tThe Adaptations for Thermoregulation in Winter Moths (for example)

- Center your name 10 lines under the title in 12-point font
- Center the date of submission, a double space below your name in 12-point font
- Center the following phrase a triple space below the date: "a paper submitted to the faculty of the Department of Biology, College of Computational Sciences, Mekelle University, Mekelle, in partial fulfillment of the requirements of Senior Seminar, Biology 401"

Pagination (giving the page number)

- Number the pages consecutively, beginning with the title page, which does not have a page number but is still counted as the first page
- Use only arabic numbers (1, 2, 3, etc.)
- Put the page numbers in the upper right hand corner

Headings

- Choose it carefully
- Make them informative and concise
- Center headings.
- Triple space before the heading and double space after the heading
- Use 12-point font, but bold

Using Numbers in Paper

- Spell out numbers less than 10 (like -ten individuals of a species, instead of 10 individuals of a species)

- Do not begin a sentence with a numeral, even if it larger than 10
- Always use numerals when reporting quantitative data with a unit: 15 km, 8 g, 5 ml (check McMillan pp. 155-157 for proper abbreviations)

Tables and Figures

- Tables and figures should be inserted in the text after its citation in the running text.
- Cite according to number: " — —as shown in Figure 3." " — — the relationships of the species (Table 2)."
- Each table and figure should be self-explanatory.
- Left justify all titles and legends (single-spaced).
- Put a period after the number of the figure or table in the title. Figure 1. Survivorship of *Xanthium strumarium* seed over a period of 100 days.
- Tables and figures should be cited according to number, "as shown in Figure 3," or "the relationships of the species (Table 2)."
- Make sure to reference figures in title, if taken from a source.
- Triple space before and after each table or figure.

Tables

- Use at least one table in a paper.
- Make sure to know when to use and when not to use. Use to present many numberical data or to summarize verbal material from text. Do not use to show patterns or trends.
- Reference table in preceding paragraph: Table 1 shows — or — — (Table1).
- Number tables consecutively throughout paper, even if there is only one.
- Always horizontally centered.
- How to set up
  - Title at top, left justified — Table 1. XXXXXXXXXXXXX (Citation 2005).

- Spanner line
- Header
- Sub-header
- Spanner
- Data
- Spanner

Figures

Anything not mentioned in a table or text can be given in the form of Figure, Graphs (Line graph, Bar diagram)

- Reference figure in preceding paragraph. Figure 1 illustrates — or — (Fig. 1)
- Number figures consecutively throughout, but separately from tables
- Always horizontally centered
- How to set up: Figure is on top. If it is a graph, make sure axes are labeled: independent variable on X-axis and dependent variable on Y-axis. If it is an illustration, include spanner lines
- Title at bottom, left justified - Figure 1. XXXXXXXXXXX (Citation 2005).
- Scientific Names should always be italized. Always italicized, Genus capitalized, species not, Abbreviate genus name after the first reference: *Querus alba* becomes *Q. alba*, Avoid using common names without scientific names, Do not use articles (*the, a, an*) with scientific names, "Species" is a collective singular: There is no such word as *specie*. For example, "This species is specific to one locale."
- Taxonomic levels above the genus level are capitalized but not italicized: the Chilopoda (centipedes), Animalia, Chordata, Osteichthyes

Subscripts and Superscripts

Use superscripts for degree measurements, ion charges, and mathematical expressions: $36°C$, Ca^{++} or Ca^{+2}, $C+$, Use subscripts for chemical compounds: $CaCl_2$ $Fe_2(SO_4)_3$

8.5. ORAL PRESENTATIONS

It is important to remember that oral presentation of a paper does not constitute publication, and therefore different rules apply. The greatest distinction is that the published paper must contain the full experimental protocol, so that the experiments can be repeated. Extensive citation of the literature is also undesirable in an oral presentation.

Most oral presentations are short (with a limit of 10 minutes at many meetings). Thus, even the theoretical content must be trimmed down relative to that of a written paper. No matter how well organized, too many ideas too quickly presented will be confusing. You should stick to your most important point or result and stress that. There will not be time for you to present all your other neat ideas.

There are, of course, other and longer types of oral presentations. A typical time allotted for symposium presentations is 20 minutes. A few are longer. A seminar is normally one hour. Obviously, you can present more material if you have more time. Even so, you should go slowly, carefully presenting a few main points or themes. If you proceed too fast, especially at the beginning, your audience will lose the interest; the daydreams will begin and your message will be lost.

During oral presentation of small, informal scientific meetings, various types of visual aids may be used. Overhead projectors, flip charts, and even blackboards can be used effectively. Every scientist should know how to prepare effective slides.

Here are some of the important points to be considered while preparing slides. First, slides should be designed specifically for use with oral presentations. Slides prepared from graphs that were drawn for journal publication are not much effective and slides prepared from a word-processed manuscript or from a printed journal or book are almost never effective. It should also be remembered that slides should be wide rather than high, which is just the opposite of the preferred dimensions for printed illustrations. Thus, horizontally oriented slides are usually preferable.

Second, slides should be prepared by professionals or at least by using professional equipment. Word processing is fine if a large type size is selected. Your graphs should be computer generated.

Third, it should be remembered that the lighting in meeting rooms is seldom optimum for slides. Contrast is therefore important. The best (most readable) slides have black text on a white background.

Fourth, slides should not be crowded. Each slide should be designed to illustrate a particular point or perhaps to summarize a few. If a slide cannot be understood in 4 seconds, it is a bad slide.

Fifth, go to the hall ahead of the audience. Check the projector, the advance mechanism and the lights.

Normally, each slide should make one simple, easily understood visual statement. The slide should supplement what you are saying at the time the slide is on the screen; the slide should not simply repeat what you are saying. And you should never read the slide text to the audience; to do so would be an insult to your audience, unless you are addressing a group of illiterates. Slides that are thoughtfully designed and well prepared can greatly enhance the value of a scientific presentation. Poor slides may dent your impression and ruined off valuable time of audience.

The Audience

The presentation of a paper at a scientific meeting is a two-way process. Because the material being communicated at a scientific conference is likely to be the newest available information in that field, both the speakers and the audience should accept certain obligations. As indicated above, speakers should present their material clearly and effectively so that the audience can understand and learn from the information being communicated.

Almost certainly, the audience for an oral presentation will be more diverse than the readership of a scientific paper. Therefore, the oral presentation should be more general level than be a written paper. Avoid technical detail. Define terms. Explain difficult concepts. A bit of redundancy can be very helpful.

To make communication more effective, the audience also has various responsibilities. These start with simple courtesy. The audience should be quiet and attentive. Speakers respond well to an interested, attentive audience, whereas the communication process can be virtually destroyed when the audience is noisy or, worse, asleep.

The best part of an oral presentation is often the question-and-answer period. The speaker has an obligation to be considerate (to take care) to the audience, and the audience has an obligation to be considerate to the speaker.

Regardless of the medium you choose, organization of your topic is the key. Each slide should be designed to cover one major point, with a bulleted text listing no more than six subtopics related to it. The main heading should be at least 20 to 24 points, with subtopics no smaller than 16 points. If the room in which you are presenting is large, use larger font sizes. When a table or graph is used, list it by name and set all the type in at least 14 points, so that it can be read at a distance. Do not clutter the page with more topics and subheads beyond the heading and the name of the graphic.

When you are working with color, decide on a color scheme before you start to worry about readability and effect within a presentation. Readability is all important. The text must stand out from your background, and good contrast between the background and your text will allow for that. If you choose a dark color for the text, use a light, soft color for background elements. A good combination is a soft yellow background with bright dark blue text. Bullets can be set in a darker blue. This color combination will provide good printouts for audience distribution. If you want to use a dark background, such as a dark gray or navy blue, the type and other elements should be white, pale yellow, or some other pale color. This color combination will look good on the screen, but it will not provide the best handouts. Be aware, however, that it is easy to overdo the color effects and ruin an otherwise good presentation.

Consistent use of color will add a cohesive quality to your presentation. If you use the same color consistently for each element throughout the slide presentation, it will communicate your ideas without confusion. For example, if you are using dark-blue bullets in a standard bullet shape, don't change the shape to a triangle midway through the presentation. Changing the color midway through a presentation would be even worse. Your viewer will wonder why you have made the change and unconsciously look for the reason even when there is none. Templates usually provide a color scheme that works well. If you don't like the design of a template, but like the colors, use them as part of a slide layout you do like. To conclude your presentation, add a black slide; it's what the professional do. Yoy can also use visual effects or animations.

What is Important in a Presentation?

- Words
- Voice
- Body language

The most important = NON verbal

- Words 10% (content)

- Voice 40%
- Body 50% (face expressions)

Structure the presentation

- Scenario
- Sequence of data, idea
- Presentation 20%
- Preparation 80%

Composition of the slides

- 1 idea per slide
- 6 words per line
- 6 lines per slide
- Simple
- Clear

Composition of the slides

- First visual effect
- Simple words,
- Rounded figures
- Explain visual items
- Text comes afterwards
- Short sentences
- Style 'telegram'
- Light page layout
- Bring the essential items
- Text - Let it appear .... line by line
- Sober background
- Finish a slide with strength

Letter type

- As homogeneous as possible

- Lower case better than Caps (capital letters)
- Max. 1 or 2 letter types
- Max.3 sizes of letters (min. 22 p.)

Character choice

- Italic to indicate a difference
- Bold or underlined to indicate the importance
- Put enough distance between sentences
- Avoid too much centering

Use of colours

- Pay attention to contrast background / text

Keep enough white and empty space

- The presentation should, breathe
- Provide animation, but don't make the audience dizzy

8.6. POSTER PRESENTATION

Posters are display boards on which scientists show their data and describe their experiments. In recent years, poster displays have become more common at both national and international meetings. With the increase in number of participants, pressure has mounted on program committees to schedule more and more papers for oral presentation, which is very difficult to manage. If organizing committee is going to include all papers for oral presentation, committee has to arrange large size auditorium and more days to accommodate all papers that may put extra burden on budget. It may also become difficult or impossible for participants to attend oral presentation of all scientist/colleagues. Therefore, just to reduce all these inconvenience and pressure, organizing committee also arrange option for poster presentation. The organization of a poster normally follows the IMRAD format. In a well-designed poster, very little *text* is used and most of the space being used for illustrations. The Introduction should present the problem concisely. The poster will fail unless it has a clear statement of purpose right at the beginning. The Methods section will be very brief; perhaps just a sentence or two will suffice to describe the type of approach used. The Results, which is often the shortest part of a written paper, is usually the major part of a well-designed poster. Most of the available space will be used to illustrate Results. The Discussion should be brief. Some of the best posters did not even use the heading "Discussion"; instead, the heading "Conclusions" appeared over the far-right panel, the individual conclusions perhaps being in the form of numbered short sentences. Literature citations should be kept to a minimum.

Preparing the Poster

You should number your poster to agree with the program of the meeting. The title should be short and attention-grabbing. If it is too long, it might not fit on the display stand. The title should be readable out to a distance of 10 feet (3 m). The typeface should be bold and black, and the type should be about 30 mm high. The names of the authors should be somewhat smaller (perhaps 20 mm). The text type should be about 4 mm high (A type size of 24 points is suitable for text). Tahoma letters are an excellent alternative, especially for headings. Computers can produce display-size type.

A poster should be self-explanatory, allowing different viewers to proceed at their own pace. If the author has to spend most of his or her time merely explaining the poster rather than responding to scientific questions, the poster is largely a failure.

Lots of white space throughout the poster is important. Distracting mess will drive people off. Try to make it very clear what is meant to be looked at first, second, etc. Visual impact is particularly critical in a poster session. If you lack graphic talent, consider getting the help of a graphic artist. Such a professional can produce an attractive poster either in the traditional board-mounted style or in the newer single-unit photographic reproduction.

A poster should contain *highlights*, so that passersby can easily discern whether the poster is something of interest to them. If they are interested, there will be plenty of time to ask questions about the details. Also, it is a good idea to prepare handouts containing more detailed information; they will be appreciated by colleagues with similar specialties.

A poster may actually be better than an oral presentation for showing the results of a complex experiment. In a poster, you can organize the highlights of the several threads well enough to give informed viewers the chance to recognize what is going on and then get the details if they so desire. The oral presentation, is better for getting across a single result or point.

The really nice thing about posters is the variety of illustrations that can be used. There is no bar (as there often is in journal publication) to the use of color. All kinds of photographs, graphs, drawings, paintings, X-rays, and even cartoons can be presented.

Two contrasting examples

Good   Bad

Excellent posters: Some scientists do indeed have considerable creative ability. It is obvious that these people are proud of the science they are doing and that they are pleased to put it all into a pretty picture.

Terrible posters: A few were simply badly designed. The great majority of *bad* posters are bad because the author is trying to present too much. Huge blocks of typed material, especially if the type is small, will not be read. Crowds will gather around the simple, well-illustrated posters and the cluttered, wordy posters will be ignored.

Why not Oral Presentation?

Because it has:

- Time restrictions
- Limited time for discussion
- Varied audience
- Difficult to keep attention
- Many distractions

Why Poster Presentation

Because it has:

- Time for discussion

- Specific audience with high level of interest
- Personal contact
- Use as display

Your audience for poster?

- Those who work in the *same area-*
- Those who work in a *similar area*
- Who are familiar with your work
- Those who work in a *different area*

Top characteristics

- Attractive
- Interesting
- Legible

Most important items

- TITLE: attractive
- AIM or OBJECTIVES: motivation
- CONCLUSION: most important outcome

Poster design

- Horizontal (landscape) - vertical (portrait)
- Colour: - highlight information
            - do not exaggerate
- Use visuals: graphs, tables, illustrations
- Use shapes
- Use bullets
- Use simple font (comic sans, arial, bold)
- Use large font size
  - Author(s): 48 - 72 pt
  - Affiliation{s): 36 - 48 pt
  - Text: 36 - 50 pt (1.5 - 2 m)

- Use upper/lower case
- Title: 72 -120 pt (5 - 10 m)
- Headings: 48 - 80 pt
- Acknowledgements: 18 pt

Spacing

- Verify the poster dimensions (portrait / landscape)
- Blank space is important 4 to 6 separate modules
- Guide the reader through the poster by numbers, arrows, etc.: TBLR, 1. 2. 3. 4. →

Tables and Figures

Keep them simple

Common Fonts

Arial, Comic sans, Times new roman, Palantino, linotype, Bookman old style. Organize poster in IMRAD format

No need of abstract

I = Introduction with objectives
M = Materials and methods
R = Results
A = and
D = Discussion

You can also put Conclusions

There is a no need of references (or keep it minimum)

Spatial Organisation

Reading sequence: TBLR (Top, Bottom, Left, Right)
Sequence:

- Center top: Title, Name, Affiliation
- Bottom left: Materials and methods
- Top left: Objectives
- Bottom right: Table or figure
- Top right: Results
- Bottom centre: Conclusions

Scientific Communication

Poster layout

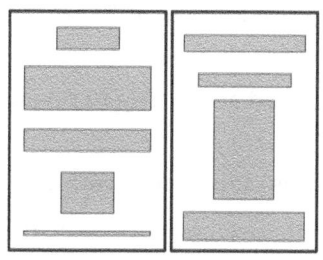
Symmetric balance

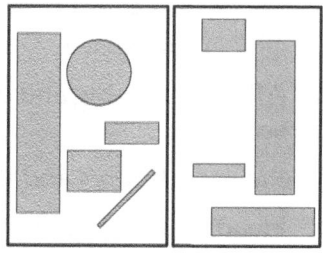
Asymetric balance

Radial balance

You as presenter

Do

- Know your subject
- Nice appearance
- Be friendly
- Be Professional
- Display your photo
- Have business cards

- Hand carry poster
- The layout should contain about 20% text, 40% graphics and 40% empty space
- All letters are big and differentiated according to position and section
- Pictures, figures and illustrations dominate visually
- Headings, text, graphic elements are large to be visible from a distance of two meters
- Background is (absent) but sections are divided hierarchically with blocks, columns and sizes of text
- The poster is supplied with cues to help readers follow your presentation
- The poster is broken up into sections, much like a scientific article

Don't

- Be distracted
- Be discouraged by lack of audience
- Leave your poster
- Ship your poster
- Forget pins, tape
- There is too much text in the poster
- Text printed uniformly with small letters of about 10-12-point font
- Visuals are on a dark background and take place in a random way
- All text and graphic elements are run into each other and are small, that does not allow to be legible or have a good look
- Background too bright or too dark, the text in one block is light
- Very difficult to identify the most important points of the poster and the viewers have no idea of organizational flow
- The poster is long, meandering the reader.

8.7. ETHICS IN RESEARCH

We are going through a time of profound change in our understanding of the ethics of applied research. After World War II a gradual consensus are developing about the key ethical principles that should underlie the research efforts. The Nuremberg War Crimes Trial following World War II brought to public view the ways German scientists had used captive human subjects of experiments. In the 1950s and 1960s, the Tuskegee Syphilis Study involved the withholding of known effective treatment for syphilis from African-American participants who were infected. Events like these forced the re-examination of ethical standards and the gradual development of a consensus that potential human subjects needed to be protected from being used as 'guinea pigs' in scientific research.

Ethical Issues

There are a number of key phrases that describe the system of ethical protections. The social and medical research establishments are showing concern to protect rights of their research participants. The principle of *voluntary participation* requires that people not be forced into participating in research. This is especially relevant where researchers had previously relied on 'captive audiences' for their subjects - prisons, universities, and places like that. Closely related to the notion of voluntary participation is the requirement of *informed consent*. Essentially, this means that prospective research participants must be fully informed about the procedures and risks involved in research and must give their consent to participate. Ethical standards also require that researchers not put participants in a situation where they might be at *risk of harm* as a result of their participation. Harm can be defined as both physical and psychological. There are two standards that are applied in order to help protect the privacy of research participants. Almost all research guarantees the participants about *confidentiality* - they are assured that identifying information will not be made available to anyone who is not directly involved in the study. The stricter standard is the principle of *anonymity* which essentially means that the participant will remain anonymous throughout the study - even to the researchers themselves. Clearly, the anonymity standard is a stronger guarantee of privacy, but it is sometimes difficult to accomplish, especially in situations where participants have to be measured at multiple time points (e.g., a pre-post study). Increasingly, researchers have had to deal with the ethical issue of a person's *right to service*. When a treatment or program may have beneficial effects, participants may get rights for equal access to services.

There is a need to establish a procedure that assures that researchers will consider all relevant ethical issues in formulating research plans. To address such needs institutions and organizations must formulate an *Institutional Review Board (IRB)*, a panel of persons who reviews grant proposals with respect to ethical implications and decides whether additional actions need to be taken to assure the safety and rights of participants. By reviewing proposals for research, IRBs also help to protect both the organization and the researcher against potential legal implications of neglecting to address important ethical issues of participants.

Plagiarism

Plagiarism derives from Latin *plagiârius*, "kidnapper", equivalent to *plagium*, "kidnapping". *Plagiarism*, as defined in the 1995 *Random House Compact Unabridged Dictionary*, is the "use or close imitation of the language and thoughts of another author and the representation of them as one's own original work."Within academia, plagiarism by students, professors, or researchers is considered academic dishonesty or academic fraud, and offenders are subject to academic censure, up to and including expulsion. Some individuals caught plagiarizing in academic contexts claim that they plagiarized unintentionally, by failing to include quotations or give the appropriate citation. While plagiarism in academics has a centuries-old history, the development of the Internet, where articles appear as electronic text, has made the physical act of copying the work of others much easier.

Many students feel pressured to complete papers well and quickly. With the accessibility of new technology (the Internet) students can plagiarize by copying and pasting information from other sources. This is often easily detected by teachers for several reasons. First, students' choices of sources are frequently unoriginal; instructors may receive the same passage copied from a popular source from several students. Second, it is often easy to tell whether a student used his or her own "voice." Third, students may choose sources which are inappropriate, inaccurate, or off-topic. Fourth, lecturers may insist that submitted work is first submitted to an online plagiarism detector.

In the academic world, plagiarism by students is a very serious offense that can result in punishments such as a failing grade on the particular assignment or for the course .For cases of repeated plagiarism, or for cases in which a student commits severe plagiarism (e.g., submitting a copied piece of writing as original work), a student may be suspended or expelled. In many universities, academic degrees or awards may be revoked as a penalty for plagiarism. Recent use of plagiarism detection software gives a more accurate picture of this activity's prevalence.For professors and researchers, plagiarism is punished by sanctions ranging from suspension to termination, along with the loss of credibility and integrity. Charges of plagiarism against students and professors are typically heard by internal disciplinary committees, which students and professors have agreed to be bound by.

Self-plagiarism

Self-plagiarism (also known as "recycling fraud" is the reuse of significant, identical, or nearly identical portions of one's own work without acknowledging that one is doing so or without citing the original work. Articles of this nature are often referred to as duplicate or multiple publications. In addition to the ethical issue, this can be illegal if copyright of the prior work has been transferred to another entity. Typically, self-plagiarism is only considered to be a serious ethical issue in settings where a publication is asserted to consist of new material, such as in academic publishing or educational assignments. It does not apply (except in the legal sense) to public-interest texts, such as social, professional, and cultural opinions usually published in newspapers and magazines. In academic fields, self-plagiarism is when an author reuses portions of their own published and copyrighted work in subsequent publications, but without attributing the previous publication. Identifying self-plagiarism is often difficult because limited reuse of material is both legally accepted (as fair use) and ethically accepted. It is common for university researchers to rephrase and republish their own work, preparing it for different academic journals and newspaper articles. However, it must be borne in mind that these researchers also obey limits. If half an article is the same as a previous one, it will usually be rejected. One of the functions of the process of peer review in academic writing is to prevent this type of "recycling".

8.8. COMMONLY MISUSED WORDS

The following list of commonly misused words was initially prepared by the Iowa Experiment Station Publications at Iowa State University, and was modified by the editors of the Journal of Mammalogy.

ABOVE - (the above method, as mentioned above) - often used in reference to something preceding, but not necessarily above; a loose reference, convenient to writers but not for readers. Also, remember that if something was mentioned previously, to do so again is redundant.

ACCURATE - (an accurate estimate) - accurate implies complete freedom from error or absolute exactness. An estimate is an approximation. Try "a reliable estimate."

AFFECT, EFFECT - Affect is a verb that means to influence. Effect, as a verb, means to bring about; as a noun, effect means result.

ALIQUOT - aliquot means "contained an exact number of times in another." Commonly misused to mean subsample.

ALL OF, BOTH OF - Just 'all' or 'both' will suffice.

ALSO SEE - (also see Jones 1950) - Often unnecessary.

ALTERNATE, ALTERNATIVE - alternate implies occurring in succession or every other one; alternative implies a choice among two or more incompatible objects, situations, or courses of action.

AMONG - used when comparing more than two items.

AND/OR - use one or the other.

AND THEN - use one or the other.

APPARENTLY, APPARENT - means obviously, clearly, plainly evident, seemingly, ostensibly and observably. Consider using one of these more specific terms.

APPEAR - not synonymous with seems. He always appears on the scene, but never seems to know what to do.

AS - do not use to mean because, or in as much as.

AS WELL AS - =and.

AT THE PRESENT TIME, AT THIS POINT IN TIME - =now.

BELOW - (see 'above'; direction does not change ambiguity).

BETWEEN - used when comparing only two items.

BY MEANS OF - just 'by'.

CARRIED OUT - colloquial; use 'conducted', 'performed' or 'was studied'.

CASE - if necessary, use 'in this instance'.CHECKED - (The traps were checked). imprecise. use 'examined' or another more precise word.

Scientific Communication

COMPARE WITH, COMPARE TO - 'compare with' means to examine differences and similarities; 'compare to' means to represent as similar. Usually, one compares with or contrasts to.

COMPRISE - means to contain or include, not constitute. "The whole comprises the parts; the parts do not comprise the whole."

DATA - plural. These data, data were, too few data.

"DIFFER FROM, DIFFER WITH - One thing differs from another, although you may differ with a colleague.

DIFFERENT THAN - never always DIFFERENT FROM.

DUE TO - implies causality when only a relationship may be intended. Try 'related to' or, if causality is intended, 'because of'.

DURING THE COURSE OF, IN THE COURSE OF - just 'during' and 'in' will usually suffice.

EITHER...OR, NEITHER...NOR - apply to no more than two items or categories; similarly, former and latter refer to the first and last of only two items or categories.

EQUALLY AS GOOD, EQUALLY AS GOOD AS - 'equally good'.

ETC. - avoid entirely

FELT - (it was felt that...) - One feels cloth, but believes ideas.

GIVEN - (at a given time) - fixed, specified or specific are more precise. Given has numerous meanings.

HIGH(ER), LOW(ER) - Commonly used imprecisely or ambiguously for greater, less, larger, smaller, more, or fewer.

HOWEVER - do not use with another conjunction at the beginning of a sentence or independent clause ('However, because...' or 'However, since...').

IN FACT, AS A MATTER OF FACT - usage tends to weaken preceding and subsequent statements by implying that they might be less than factual. If a lead word is needed, try 'indeed'.

IN ORDER TO - 'To' will suffice.

IN VIEW OF THE FACT THAT - 'because'.

INTERESTING, INTERESTING TO NOTE - presumption; let the reader decide what is interesting.

IRREGARDLESS - no such word   Use regardless or irrespective.

IT SHOULD BE MENTIONED, NOTED, POINTED OUT, EMPHASIZED - delete completely and make the point emphatically

IT WAS FOUND, DETERMINED, DECIDED - delete, and state observation declaratively.

LESS(ER), FEW(ER) - 'less' refers to quantity, 'few' refers to number.

NON - a prefix, usually not hyphenated. Avoid overuse. 'Non' defines things negatively and is not descriptive of what they are. Do not use as a substitute for established prefixes or where 'not...' will serve. (incorrect, unreliable, not reliable).

ONCE, WHEN - avoid the use of 'once' for 'when', as 'once' can mean: one time, formerly, simultaneously, and immediately.

OUT, IN - (...14 out of 17; to find out if) - in most instances, these can be omitted without altering meaning.

PARTIALLY, PARTLY - 'partially' implies bias in favor of one or the other. Partly is more precise when portion or proportion is meant.

PERCENT, PERCENTAGE - use percent (%) with numbers, use percentage in reference to proportion expressed in hundredths.

PREDOMINATE, PREDOMINANT - predominate is a verb, predominant is an adjective. The adverb is predominantly, not predominately.

PREVALENCE, INCIDENCE - prevalence is the number per unit of population at a specific time (23 per 1000 individuals in 1989). Incidence is number in a population per unit time (23 cases per year).

PRIOR TO, PREVIOUS TO - adjectives that modify nouns; prior or previous events. Replace 'prior to' or 'previous to' with 'before'.

PROVEN - be careful of this word; rarely is anything proven in science. We test hypotheses and sometimes fail to reject one, but this is not proof.

PROVIDED, PROVIDING - 'provided that' is a conjunction; providing is the participle.

RESPECTIVE, RESPECTIVELY - omit if possible.

SAID - (Jones (1978) said that...) - use wrote, noted suggested or some other term, as nothing was 'said'.

SINCE - denotes a relationship in time. Do not use as a synonym for because.

SMALL IN SIZE, RECTANGULAR IN SHAPE, GREEN IN COLOR redundant in repetition.

TAXA AND VERB AGREEMENT - species and subspecies take singular verbs whereas genera and higher taxa take plural verbs. Peromyscus maniculatus is common in northern Illinois. Peromyscus are widely distributed in North America.

THAT, WHICH - two words that can help, when needed, to make intended meanings and relationships unmistakable, which often is important in scientific writing. If the clause can be omitted without leaving the modified noun incomplete, use which and enclose the clause within commas or parentheses; otherwise use that.

THIS, THESE - commonly used to begin sentences when the antecedents to which they refer are unclear. 'Elephants, whales, and bats are mammals although bats fly like birds. These animals are endothermic.' Mammals? Birds? Mammals and Birds?

TO BE - (the differences were found to be significant) - frequently unnecessary.

TO SEE - replace with 'to determine' or another more precise term.

TOTAL - (a total of ten squirrels were observed) - usually superfluous.

UTILIZE, UTILIZATION - use

VARYING, VARIOUS, DIFFERENT, DIFFERING - commonly misused as synonyms. Varying amounts or differing conditions imply individually changing amounts or conditions rather than a selection of various amounts or different conditions.

VERY, QUITE, CONSIDERABLE, SOMEWHAT - avoid modifiers that impart indefinite measure. 'A very large bear' is as undefined in size as a 'large bear'.

VIABLE ALTERNATIVE - it would not be an alternative if it were not viable.

WHERE - implies a locality; do not use as a synonym for 'in which'.

8.9. SUMMARY

Research outcome may be communicated in the following forms
- Thesis
- Scientific research paper communicated to journals
- Review paper
- Oral presentations ·
- Poster presentation

Ethics
- Conducting and publication of research has certain ethics

Chapter – 9

Presentation of Data

Studying this chapter will enable us:
- *To present data using tables*
- *To represent data using appropriate diagrams.*
- *To know how to estimate sample size for testing equality of two Proportion*
- *To know how to estimate sample size for control study*
- *To know how to estimate sample size for comparing two Population Mean*

9.1. INTRODUCTION

A data are generally voluminous, so they need to be put in a compact and presentable form. This chapter deals with presentation of data precisely so that the voluminous data collected could be made usable readily and are easily comprehended. There are generally three forms of presentation of data:
  I. Textual or Descriptive presentation
  II. Tabular presentation
  III. Diagrammatic presentation

9.2. TEXTUAL PRESENTATION OF DATA

In textual presentation, data are described within the text. When the quantity of data is not too large this form of presentation is more suitable. We can see the following example:

A strike call was given on 08 September 2009 protesting the hike in prices of petrol and diesel, 15 petrol pumps were found open and 27 were closed whereas 12 schools were closed and remaining 19 schools were found open in a town.

In this case data have been presented only in the text. A serious drawback of this method of presentation is that one has to go through the complete text of presentation for comprehension but at the same time, it enables one to emphasize certain points of the presentation.

9.3. TABULAR PRESENTATION OF DATA

In a tabular presentation, data are presented in rows (horizontally) and columns (vertically). For example see Table-1. It has 3 rows (for male, female and total) and 3 columns (for urban, rural and total/average). It is called a 3 × 3 table giving 9 items of information in 9 boxes called the "cells" of the table. Each cell gives information that relates an attribute of gender ("male", "female" or total/average) with a number (literacy percentages of rural people, urban people and total). The most important advantage of tabulation is that it organises data for further statistical treatment and decision-making. Classification used in tabulation is of four kinds:

I. Qualitative
II. Quantitative
III. Temporal and
IV. Spatial

Qualitative Classification

When classification is done according to qualitative characteristics like social status, physical status, nationality, etc., it is called qualitative classification. For example, in Table-1 the characteristics for classification are sex and location which are qualitative in nature.

Table 1 : Literacy percentage by sex and location

Sex	Location		Average
	Rural	Urban	
Male	57.70	80.80	60.32
Female	30.03	63.30	33.57
Average	43.86	72.05	46.95

Table 2 : Distribution of respondent by their age in an election (**Courtesy NCERT**)

Age group	No of respondent	Percent
20-30	3	0.55
30-40	61	11.25
40-50	132	24.35
50-60	153	28.24
60-70	140	25.83
70-80	51	9.41
80-90	2	0.37
All	542	100

In quantitative classification, the data are classified on the basis of characteristics which are quantitative in nature. In other words these characteristics can be measured quantitatively. For example, age, height, production, income, etc are quantitative characteristics. See Table-2.

Temporal Classification

In this, classification is done according to time and time becomes the classifying variable. In temporal classification, data are categorized according to time. Time may be in hours, days, weeks, months, years, etc. For example, see Table-3.

Table 3: Yearly sales of a tea shop from 1995 to 2000 (Courtesy NCERT)

995	79.2
1996	81.3
1997	82.4
1998	80.5
1999	100.2
2000	91.2

In this table the classifying characteristic is year and takes values in the scale of time.

Spatial Classification

In this, classification is done on the basis of place or location. The place may be a village/town, block, district, state, country, etc. Table-4 is an example of spatial classification, where classifying characteristic is country of the world.

Table 4 : Export from India to rest of the world in one year as share of total export (per cent)

DESTINATION	EXPORT SHARE (%)
France	15
UK	5
Other EU	21
Germany	2
China	5
Russia	6
Other East Europe	1
OPEC	11
Asia	20
Africa	5
Others	9
All	100

Arrangement of Data in Tabular Form

To construct a table, it is important to put all parts together in a systematic manner. The simplest way of conceptualizing a table may be data presented in rows and columns along with some explanatory notes. A good table should essentially have the following:

Table Number

For identification purpose, number is assigned to a table. It is given at the top or at the beginning of the title of the table. Table numbers are whole numbers in ascending order. Subscripted numbers like 1.2, 3.1, etc. are also in use for identifying the table according to its chapter (Table-5).

Title

The title of a table narrates about the table. It should be very clear and brief. It finds place at the head of the table succeeding the table number or just below it (Table-5).

Column Headings

At the top of each column in a table a column designation is given. This is called caption or column heading (Table-5).

Stubs or Row Headings

Like a column heading, each row of the table has to be given a heading. The designations of the rows are also called stubs or stub items, and the complete left column is known as stub column. A brief description of the row headings may also be given at the left hand top in the table (Table-5).

Body of the Table

Body of a table is the main part and it contains the actual data. Location of any one figure/data in the table is fixed and determined by the row and column of the table. For example, data in the second row and fourth column indicate that 25 crore females in rural India were non-workers in 2001 (Table-5).

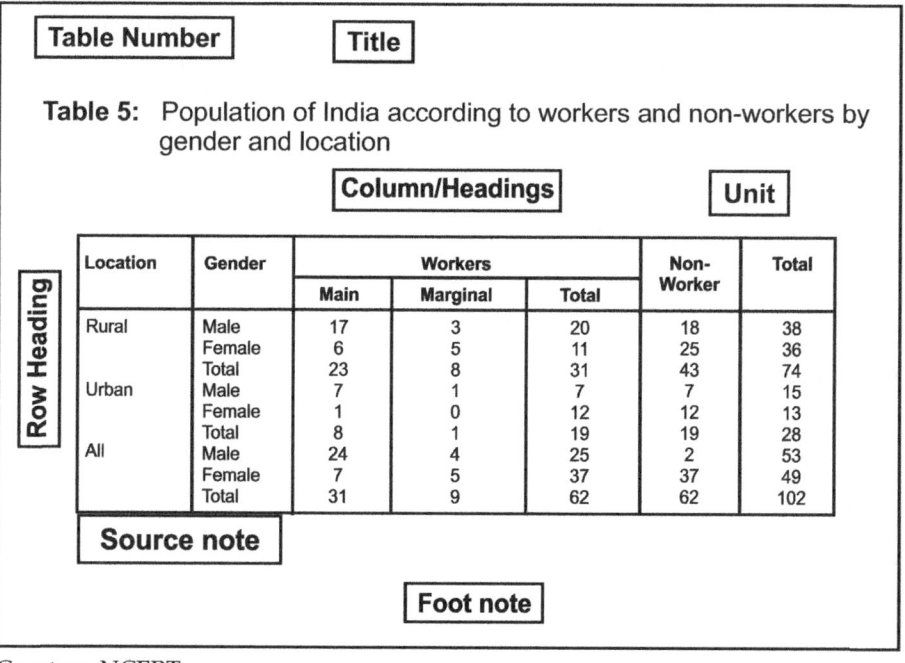

Courtesy NCERT

Unit of Measurement

The unit of measurement of the figures in the table should always be stated along with the title. If figures are large, they should be rounded up and the method of rounding should be indicated.

Source Note

It is a brief statement or phrase indicating the source of data presented in the table. If more than one source is there, all the sources are to be written in the source note. Source note is generally written at the bottom of the table (Table-5).

Footnote

Footnote is the last part of the table and it explains the specific feature of the data content of the table which is not self explanatory and has not been explained earlier.

9.4. DIAGRAMMATIC PRESENTATION OF DATA

This is another way of presenting a data. This method provides the quickest understanding of the actual situation. Diagrammatic presentation of data depicts quite effectively. Diagrams may be less accurate but are much more effective than tables in presenting the data.

Commonly following types of diagrams are used for the purpose:

(i)   Geometric diagram

(ii) Frequency diagram

(iii) Arithmetic line graph

Geometric Diagram

Bar diagram and pie diagram are categorised under geometric diagram for presentation of data. The bar diagrams are of three types; simple, multiple and component bar diagrams.

Bar Diagram

Simple bar diagram

Bar diagram comprises of a group of rectangular bars for each class or category of data. Each bar is equispaced and equiwidth, where height or length of the bar reads the magnitude of data. The lower end of the bar touches the base line such that the height of a bar starts from the zero units. Bars of a bar diagram can be visually compared by their relative height. Bar diagrams are more convenient for non-frequency data such as income expenditure profile, export/imports over the years, etc.

Discrete variables like family size, spots on a dice, grades in an examination, etc. and attributes such as gender, religion, caste, country, etc. can be represented by bar diagrams.

Simple bar diagrams are very popular in practice. A bar chart can be either vertical or horizontal; vertical bars are more popular.

Table 6 : The following table gives the birth rate per thousand of different countries over a certain period of time.

Country	Birth rate	Country	Birth rate
Pakistan	33	China	40
USA	15	Japan	30
Uganda	20	Oman	15

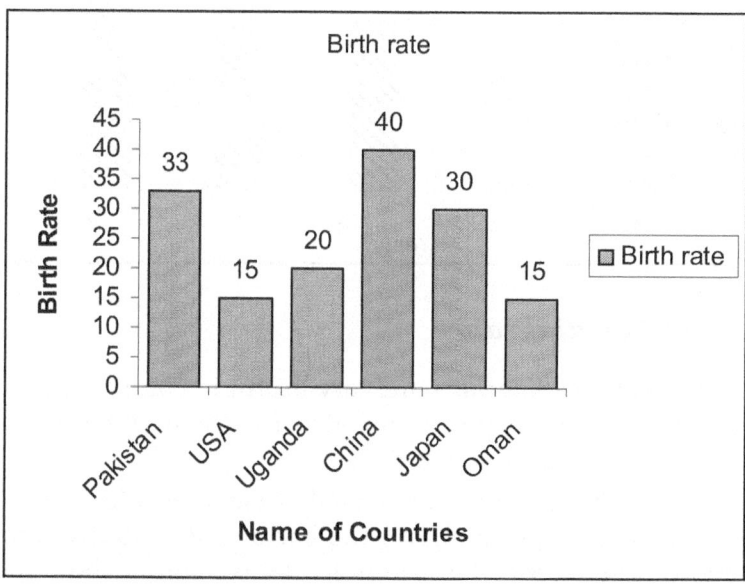

Comparing the size of bars, we can easily see that China's birth rate is the highest while USA and Oman equal in the lowest positions.

Multiple bar diagram

Multiple bar diagrams are used for comparing two or more sets of data to show them on same figure. For example if we want to show import and export for different years, it can be shown in this manner:

Years	Imports	Exports
1991	8000	4000
1992	8000	5000
1993	10000	6000
1994	11000	7000
1995	13000	8500

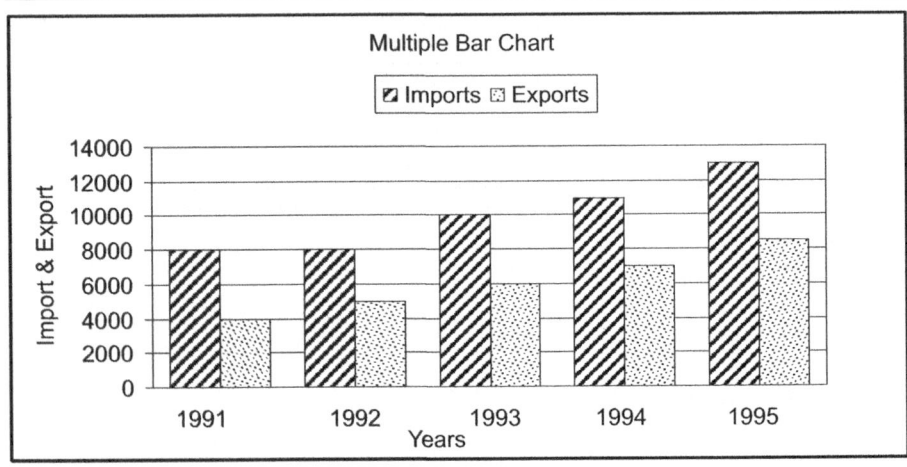

Component bar diagram

Component bar diagrams are very useful in comparing the sizes of different component parts and also for throwing light on the relationship among these integral parts.

Component bar diagrams are usually shaded or coloured suitably. A component bar diagram shows the bar and its sub-divisions into two or more components. For example, the bar might show the total production of food grains. The components show the proportion of oat, barley and wheat production in a particular year. To construct a component bar diagram, first of all, a bar is constructed on the x-axis with its height equivalent to the total value of the bar. The bar is divided into different components according to their variables.

Years	Wheat	Barley	Oats	Total
1991	34	18	27	79
1992	43	14	24	81
1993	43	16	27	86
1994	45	13	34	92

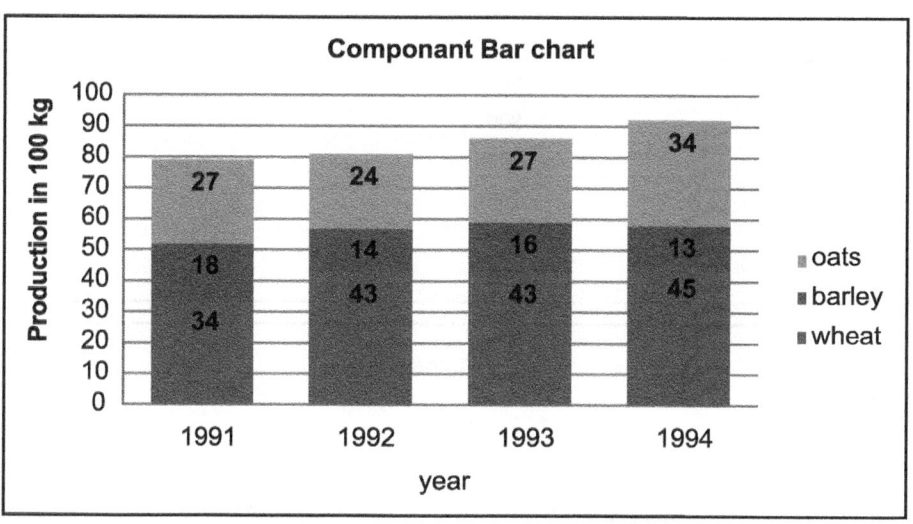

Pie Diagram or Pie Chart

A Pie diagram is also a component diagram. In this a circle's whole area is proportionally divided among the components. It is also called a pie chart. The circle is divided into as many parts as there are components by drawing straight lines from centre to the circumference.

To find the angle for each sector (component) following formula is used:

$$X^0 = \frac{\text{Value of items A}}{\text{Total value of items}} \times 360°$$

Calculation of Angle

For Food

$$= \frac{360}{7200} \times 3000$$

$$= 150^0$$

Similarly we can calculate the remaining angles, and the total of angles column should always come to 360°. While preparing the pie diagram, it is suggested to first plot variable having lowest value (lowest value of angle).

Item	Amount	Angle (in degree)
Food	3000	150
Rent	800	40
Education	1200	60
Savings	1500	75
Miscellaneous	700	35
Total	**7200**	**360**

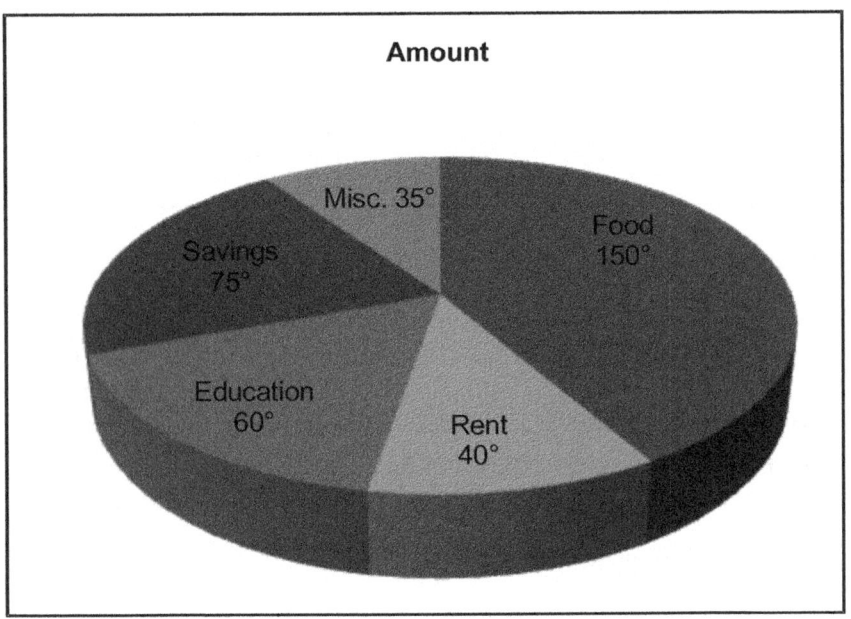

Frequency Diagram

Data in the form of grouped frequency distributions are generally represented by frequency diagrams like histogram, frequency polygon, frequency curve and ogive.

Histogram

A histogram is a two dimensional diagram. It is a set of rectangles with bases as the intervals between class boundaries (along X-axis) and width are proportional to the class frequency. If the class intervals are of equal width, which they generally are, the area of the rectangles are proportional to their respective frequencies. If the classes are not continuous they are first converted into continuous classes. Sometimes the common portion between two adjacent rectangles is omitted giving

Presentation of Data

a better impression of continuity. The resulting figure gives the impression of a double staircase.

Histogram also gives value of *mode* of the frequency distribution graphically and the x coordinate of the dotted vertical line gives the mode.

To draw a histogram, following steps are required:

(1) Marking of class intervals on X-axis and frequencies on Y-axis.

(2) The scales for both the axes need not be the same.

(3) Class intervals must be exclusive. If the intervals are in inclusive form, convert them to the exclusive form.

(4) Drawing rectangles with class intervals as bases and the corresponding frequencies as heights.

The class limits are marked on the horizontal axis and the frequency is marked on the vertical axis. Thus a rectangle is constructed on each class interval.

If the intervals are equal, then the height of each rectangle is proportional to the corresponding class frequency.

If the intervals are unequal, then the area of each rectangle is proportional to the corresponding class frequency.

Example 1

Drawing of a histogram for the following data:

CLASS INTERVAL	FREQUENCY
0-5	4
5-10	10
10-15	18
15-20	8
20-25	6

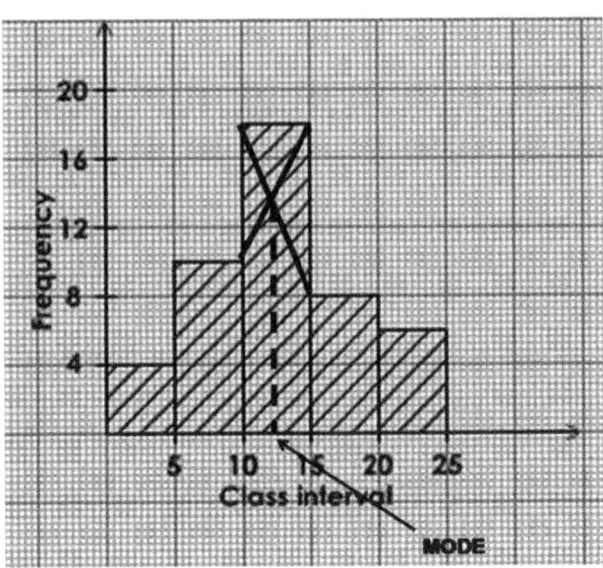

Example 2

The daily wages of 50 workers, in rupees, are given below:

In table (a), the class intervals are inclusive. So we convert them to the exclusive form as shown in table (b).

Table (a)

Wages (in Rs)	Frequency
51-60	4
61-70	12
71-80	8
81-90	16
91-100	4
101-110	6

Table (b)

Wages (in Rs)	Frequency
50.5-60.5	4
60.5-70.5	12
70.5-80.5	8
80.5-90.5	16
90.5-100.5	4
100.5-110.5	6

Answer

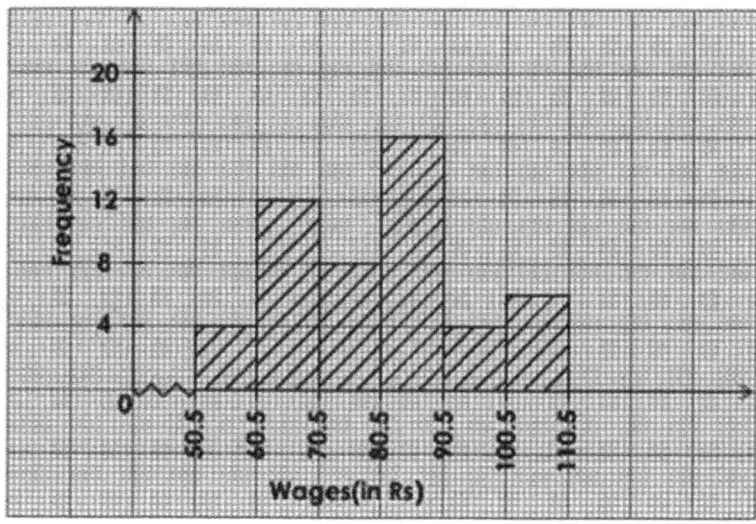

Note:

(i) The class intervals are made continuous and then the histogram is constructed.

(ii) A kink or a zig - zag curve is shown near the origin. It indicates that the scale along the horizontal axis does not start at the origin.

(iii) The horizontal scale and vertical scale need not be the same.

A histogram looks similar to a bar diagram. But there are more differences than similarities between the two than it may appear at the first impression.

Histogram	Bar Graph
1. It consists of rectangle touching each other	1. It consists of rectangle, normally separated from each other with equal space.
2. The frequency is represented by the area of each rectangle.	2. The frequency is represented by height. The width has no significance.
3. It is two dimensional (width and height are considered)	3. It is one dimensional (only height is considered)
4. It is used as a visual aid to represent data.	4. It is used as a visual aid to represent data.

Frequency polygon

Frequency polygon is an alternative to histogram and is also derived from histogram itself. A frequency polygon can be fitted to a histogram for studying the shape of the curve. The simplest method of drawing a frequency polygon is to join the midpoints of the topside of the consecutive rectangles of the histogram. It leaves us with the two ends away from the base line, denying the calculation of the area under the curve. The solution is to join the two end-points thus obtained to the base line at the mid-values of the two classes with zero frequency immediately at each end of the distribution. Broken lines or dots may join the two ends with the base line. Now the total area under the curve, like the area in the histogram, represents the total frequency or sample size.

Frequency polygon is the most common method of presenting grouped frequency distribution.

Frequency curve

In a frequency distribution, the mid-value of each class is obtained. Then on the graph paper, the frequency is plotted against the corresponding mid-value. These points are joined by straight lines. These straight lines may be extended in both directions to meet the X - axis to form a polygon.

Example-1

The weights of 50 students are recorded below. Draw a frequency polygon for this data.

Class	Mid-mark	Frequency
40-44	42	3
45-49	47	10
50-54	52	12
55-59	57	15
60-64	62	7
65-69	67	5

Suggested answer:

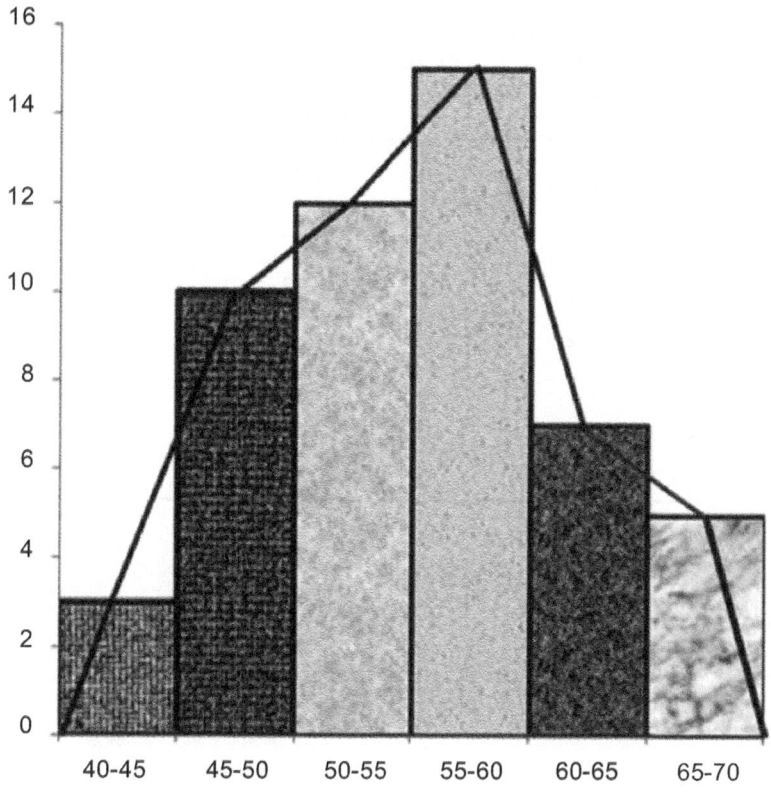

Figure: Frequency Polygon

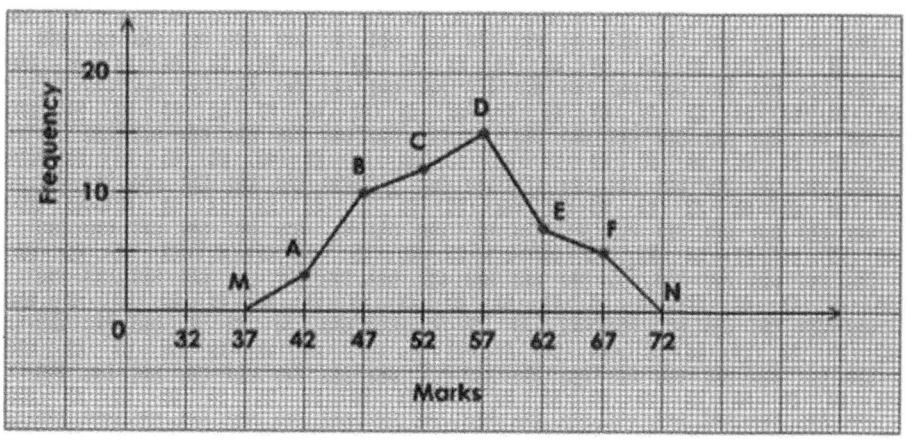

Figure: Frequency Polygon

Example 2-

The marks scored by 120 students in an examination are as given in the table form a frequency polygon.

Marks	Frequency
0-10	2
10-20	8
20-30	10
30-40	15
40-50	24
50-60	36
60-70	14
70-80	6
80-90	5

Suggested answer:

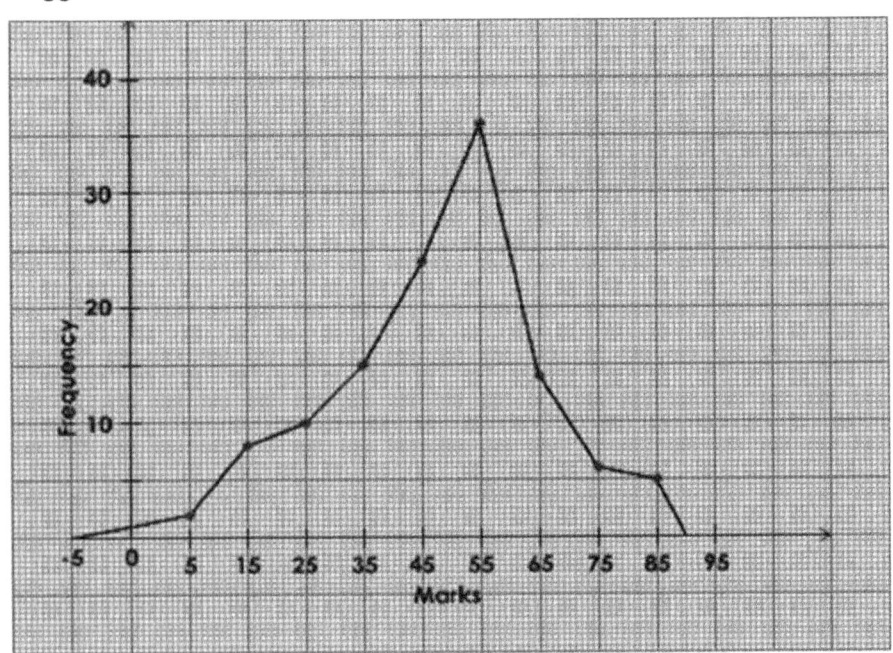

Figure: Frequency Polygon

Then frequency curve is obtained by drawing a smooth freehand curve passing through the points of the frequency polygon as closely as possible. It may not necessarily pass through all the points of the frequency polygon but it passes through them as closely as possible.

Presentation of Data

Daily earning (Rs)	No. of wage earners	Cumulative frequency	
		Less than	More than
45-49	2	2	85
50-54	3	5	83
55-59	5	10	80
60-64	3	13	75
65-69	6	19	72
70-74	7	26	66
75-79	12	38	59
80-84	13	51	47
85-89	9	60	34
90-94	7	67	25
95-99	6	73	18
100-104	4	77	12
105-109	2	79	8
110-114	3	82	6
115-119	3	85	3

Courtesy NCERT

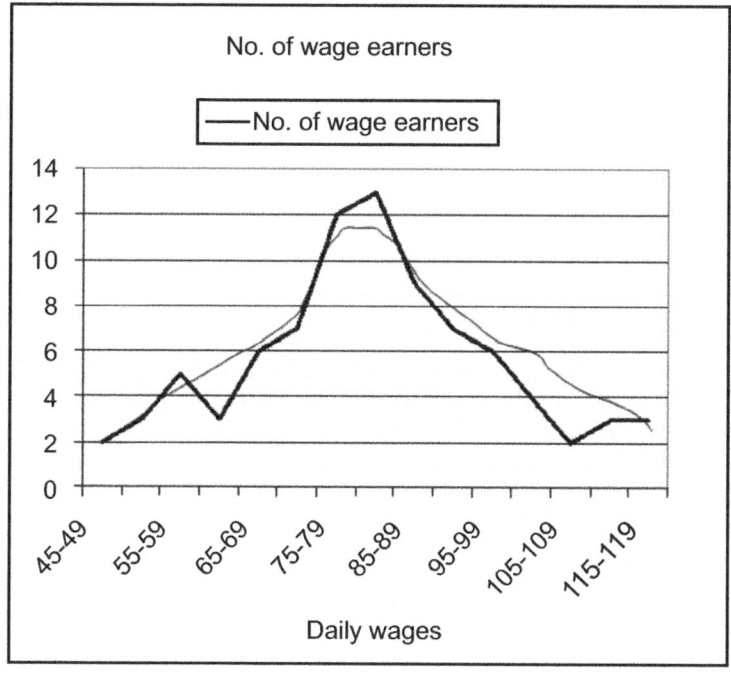

Figure : Frequency Curve

Ogive curve

Ogive is also called cumulative frequency curve. There are two types of cumulative frequencies; "less than type" and "more than type". For less than ogive the cumulative frequencies are plotted against the respective upper limits of the class intervals whereas for more than ogives the cumulative frequencies are plotted against the respective lower limits of the class interval. An interesting feature of the two ogives together is that their intersection point gives the *median* of the frequency distribution.

(i) *Less Than Ogive*:- The less than cumulative frequencies are in ascending order. The cumulative frequency of each class is plotted against the upper limit of the class interval in this type of ogive and then various points are joined by straight line.

Example:

Drawing a 'less than' ogive curve for the following data:

Marks	Frequency	Cumulative Frequency
0-10	2	2
10-20	8	10
20-30	12	22
30-40	18	40
40-50	2	68
50-60	22	90
60-70	6	96
70-80	4	100

To Plot an Ogive:

(i) We plot the points with coordinates having actual limits and ordinates as the cumulative frequencies, (10, 2), (20, 10), (30, 22), (40, 40), (50, 68), (60, 90), (70, 96) and (80, 100) are the coordinates of the points.

(ii) Join the points plotted by a smooth curve.

(iii) An Ogive is connected to a point on the X-axis representing the actual lower limit of the first class.

Scale:

X -axis 1 cm = 10 marks, Y -axis 1cm = 10 c.f.

Presentation of Data

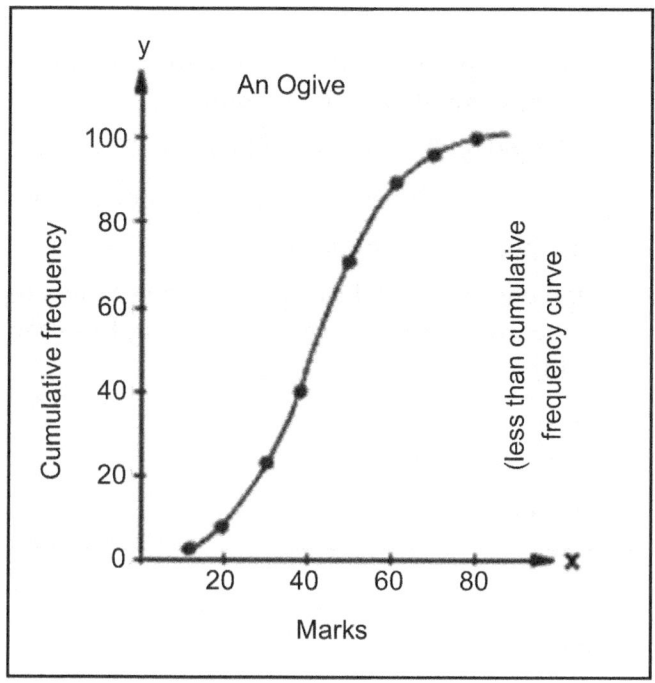

(ii) *More Than Ogive*:- The cumulative frequencies in this type are in the descending order. The cumulative frequency of each class is plotted against the lower limit of the class interval.

Example

Using the data given below, 'more than' Ogive curve is constructed.

Marks	1-10	11-20	21-30	31-40	41-50	51-60	61-70	71-80
Frequency	3	8	12	14	10	6	5	2

Marks	Frequency	Cumulative Frequency
More than 1	3	60
More than 11	8	57
More than 21	12	49
More than 31	14	37
More than 41	10	23
More than 51	6	13
More than 61	5	7
More than 71	2	2

To Plot an Ogive

(i) We plot the points with coordinates having actual lower limits and ordinates as the cumulative frequencies,

(70.5, 2), (60.5, 7), (50.5, 13), (40.5, 23), (30.5, 37), (20.5, 49), (10.5, 57), (0.5, 60) are the coordinates of the points.

(ii) Join the points by a smooth curve.

(iii) An Ogive is connected to a point on the X-axis representing the actual upper limit of the last class [in this case) i.e., point (80.5, 0)].

Scale:

X-axis 1 cm = 10 marks

Y-axis 2 cm = 10 c.f

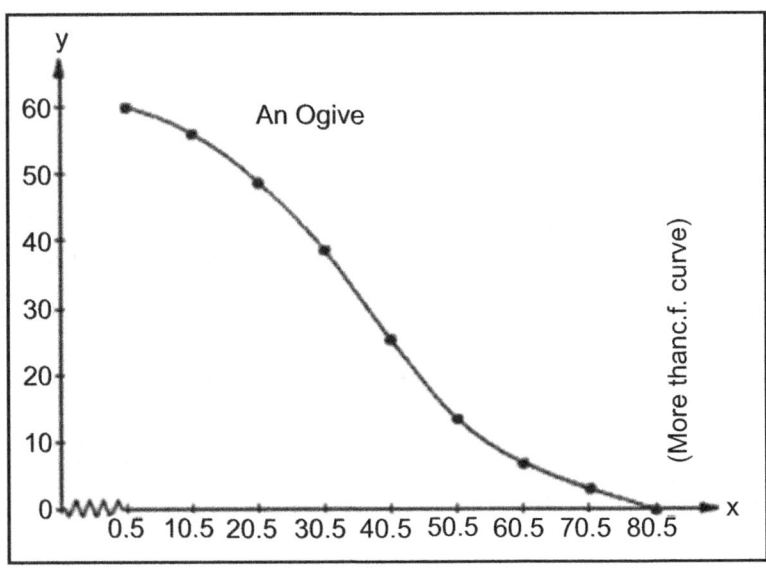

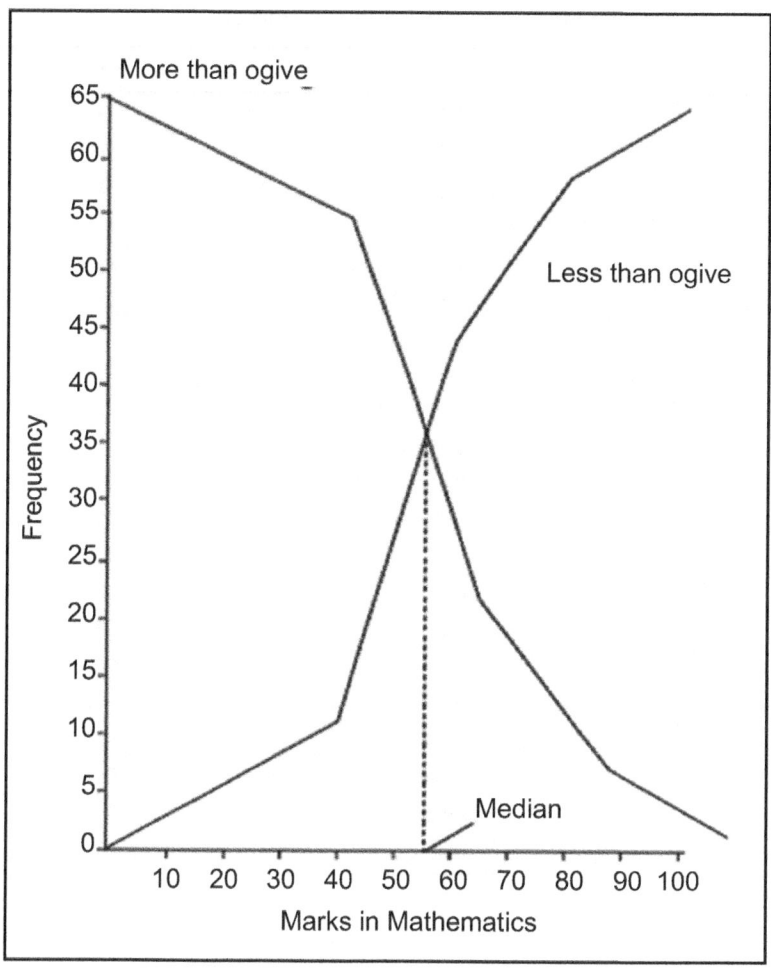

Courtesy NCERT

Arithmetic Line Graph

An arithmetic line graph is another method of diagrammatic presentation of data. In it, time (hour, day/date, week, month, year, etc.) is plotted along x-axis and the value of the variable (time series data) along y-axis. A graph line is obtained by joining these plotted points, is called arithmetic line graph (time series graph). It helps in understanding the trend, periodicity, etc. in a long term time series data. Here we can see from Fig. that for the period 1978 to 1999, although the imports were more than the exports all through, the rate of acceleration went on increasing after 1988-89 and the gap between the two (imports and exports) was widened after 1995.

Value of Export and Import of a country (Rs. in 100 crores)

Year	Exports	Imports
1977-78	54	60
1978-79	57	68
1997-80	64	91
1980-81	67	125
1982-83	88	143
1983-84	98	158
1984-85	117	171
1985-86	109	197
1986-87	125	201
1987-88	157	222
1988-89	202	282
1989-90	277	353
1990-91	326	432
1991-92	440	479
1992-93	532	634
1993-94	698	731
1994-95	827	900
1995-96	1064	1227
1996-97	1186	1369
1997-98	1301	1542
1998-99	1416	1761

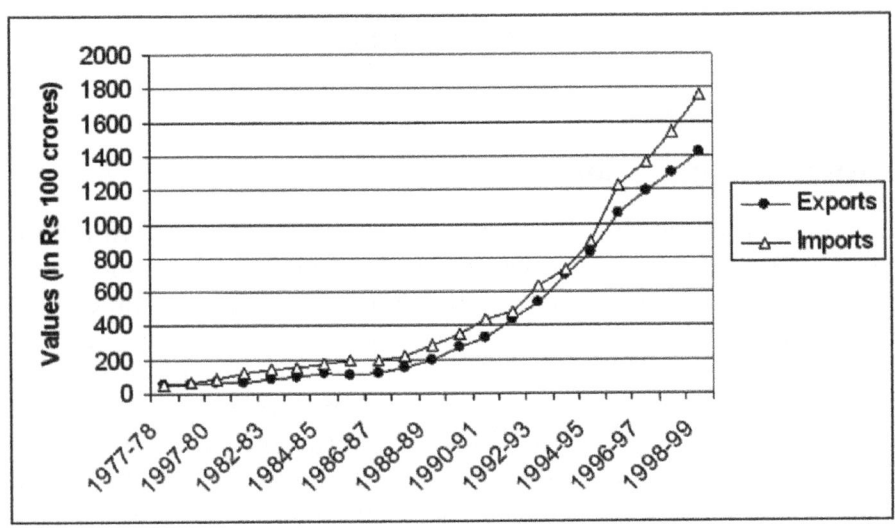

Courtesy NCERT

Presentation of Data

Stem and Leaf Plot

This is a variant of the histogram. The shape is similar to that of a histogram except that the representation in this figure is horizontal rather than vertical. Recurrence of the same values becomes easily evident in this method but intervals that are other than multiples of 10 or unequal are difficult at display. The stem and leaf plot of the systolic BP of a small group of individuals is shown below. Note that the first two digits of systolic BP is considered the 'stem' while the third digit is the 'leaf'.

Stem and	Leaf
10	8
11	238
12	00115678888999
13	0011233556667788899
14	0022568
15	231

Fig. Stem and Leaf Plot: Systolic BP of a small population

Box and Whiskers Plot

This method is used relatively frequently for variables measured in the interval/ratio scale. Two adjoining boxes are made to denote the first quartile (Q 1) and third quartile (Q3) range of observations with the median value being depicted by the contiguous side of the two boxes thus being placed one on top of the other. The vertical height of this *box* (infact 2 boxes) represents the inter quartile range. The greater the vertical height of the boxes, the greater is the spread of the observations. Vertical lines are drawn *(whiskers)* from the minimum value to the lower border of the box and also from the maximum value to the upper border of the box.

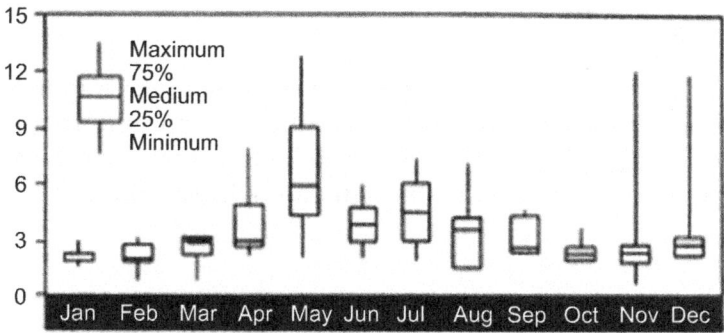

Fig : Box and Whisker plot: *E. Coli* count/100 ml water

Dendrogram

When a small number of groups, differ from each other significantly, with respect to some measurements, a special method of analysis may be employed, known as *cluster analysis*, by employing the technique of Euclidean distance. Here, groups of observation are considered together, rather than individual observations. In the first stage, two most similar entities are put into one group. In the second state, a third most similar entity is merged with the group and then analysed. This process goes on until all observations are finally merged into one big group. A dendrogram is the graphical display of the merging taking place at the various levels of hierarchical clustering.

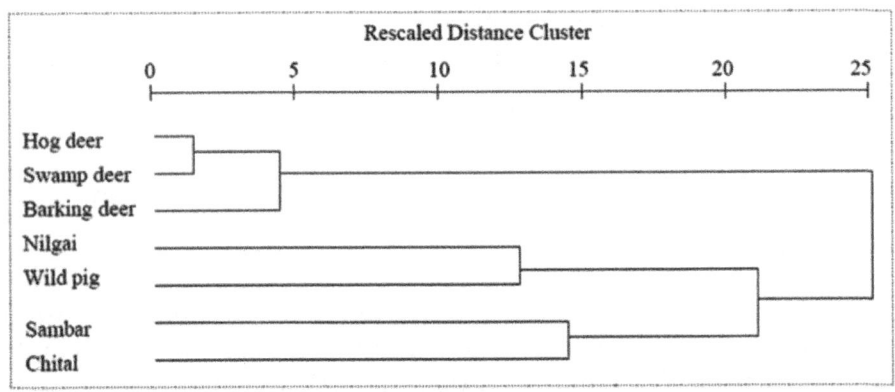

Courtesy, WII, India: Dendrogram depicting ungulates association in TAL (Ward's method)

9.5. MAPS

Maps are powerful methods used for showing the spatial distribution of a disease or health condition. Several types of maps are used by bio-medical statisticians currently. The commonly used ones are:

Spot Map

In spot map a dot is usually put to represent one or more cases. A concentration of dots in any area indicates that the incidence or prevalence of that disease condition is high in that area. This type of map is used quite frequently in epidemiological studies.

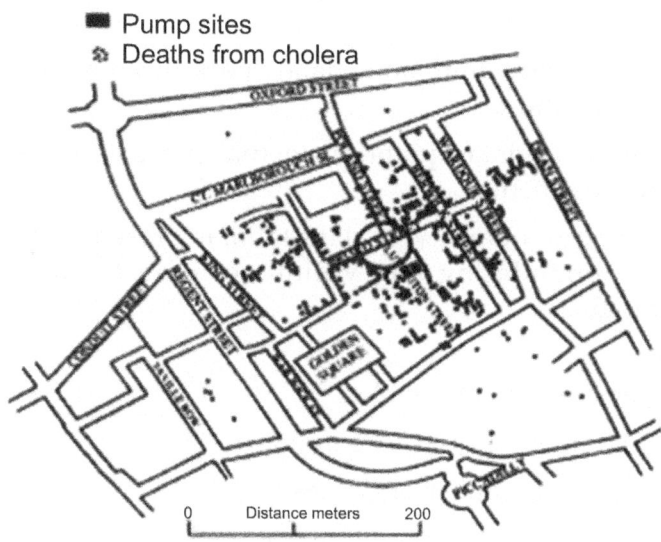

Fig. Spot map: Deaths from cholera in London (John Snow)

Thematic Choroplethic Map

In this type of map, geographical areas having similar rates are depicted in the same shade and color. The colour and shade scheme is also selected in such a way, that the shade or colour becomes darker as the rate increases.

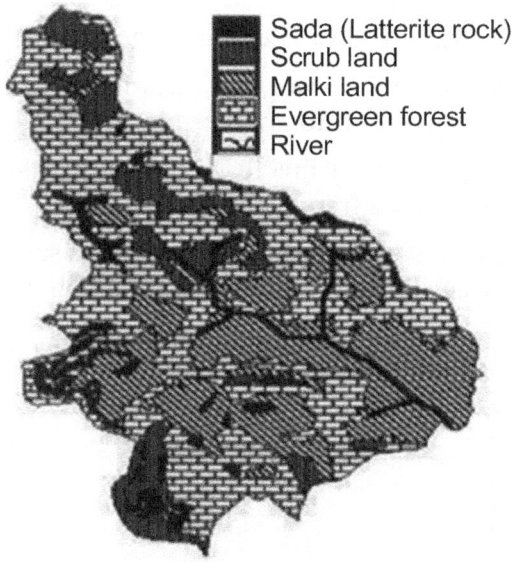

Fig : Choreplethie Map of Animal Rabies Cases (2000)

9.6. SUMMARY

- Data (even voluminous data) speak meaningfully through presentation.
- For small data (quantity) textual presentation serves the purpose better.
- For large quantity of data tabular presentation helps in accommodating any volume of data for one or more variables.

Tables

Frequency distribution table

- Class interval should be uniform
- Optimum number of classes 8-10
- Can be used for quantitative as well as qualitative data

Graphs and Diagrams

- Bar diagram: used for comparing mutually exclusive discrete data; Multiple bars, Component bars
- Histogram: variant of bar diagram; used for *continuous* or ordinal data Frequency
- Polygon: obtained by joining the mid points of the tops of the bars of a histogram
- Line diagram: shows trend 'of one variable over another.
- Scatter diagram: shows the variation in the values of one variable in relation to another
- Pie diagram: is a circle divided into segments, each representing the frequency in a category.
- Pictogram: uses pictures; each denoting a specified frequency, spatial distribution of a disease or health condition.

Chapter – 10

Bibliography

Altman, J. 1974. Observational study of behaviour: sampling methods. Behaviour.49, 227-265.

Bedekar, V. H. 1982. How to write, assignments, research papers, dissertation and theses. Kanak Publications, New Delhi. Pp. 114.

Brown, R.A. and Beck, J.S. 1990. Medical Statistics on Microcomputers. A Guide to the appropriate use of Statistical Packages. British Medical Journal, London. Pp. 103

Cochran, W. G. 1963. Sampling Technique. Asian Publishing House, Bombay. Pp. 413.

Creswell, J.W. 2008. Research Design: Qualitative, Quantitative, and Mixed Methods approaches. Sage Publications, Inc. London. Pp. 296.

Fowler, J. and Cohen, L. 1986. Statistics for Ornithology. British Trust for Ornithology.

Javed, S. and Kaul, R. 2001. Indian Bird Conservation Network (IBCN) & Bombay Natural History Society, Mumbai, India.

Koul, L. 1984. Methodology of Educational Research. Vikas Publishing House Pvt. Ltd., New Delhi. Pp. 511.

Kumar, R. 2005. Research Methodology: Sage Publication, New Delhi. Pp. 332.

Lehner, P.N. 1979. Handbook of Ethological methods. Garland STPM Press, New York & London

Page, R.M., Cole, G.E. and Timmreck, T.E. 1995. Basic Epidemiological Methods and Biostatistics: A Practical Guide Book. Jones and Bartlett Publishers. Boston, Ma.

Robert, M. Groves, Floyd, J. Fowler Jr., Mick P. Couper and James M. Lepkowski. 2009. Survey Methodology. John Wiley & Sons. NJ, USA. Pp. 488.

Singh, Y.K. 2006. Fundamental of Research Methodology and Statistics. New Age International P Limited, Publishers, New Delhi.

Vockell, E. L. 1983. Educational Research. Mac Millan Co. Inc., NY. Pp. 392.

WHO. 2001. Health Research Methodology: A guide for training in research methods. Manila, Philippines.

Printed and bound by CPI Group (UK) Ltd, Croydon, CR0 4YY
22/04/2026

14866397-0001